The Norton Scores

EIGHTH EDITION / *Volume II*

EIGHTH EDITION / *in Two Volumes*

The Norton Scores

A Study Anthology

EDITED BY

Kristine Forney

PROFESSOR OF MUSIC
California State University, Long Beach

VOLUME II:
SCHUBERT TO THE PRESENT

W · W · NORTON & COMPANY · *New York · London*

Composition by UG
Manufacturing by Courier
Book design by Antonina Krass
Cover illustration: Helmut A. Preiss, *Mandolin* (1996), collage and acrylic paint;
    collection of the artist.

ISBN 0-393-97347-6 (pbk.)

W. W. Norton & Company, Inc., 500 Fifth Avenue, New York, N.Y. 10110
http://www.wwnorton.com

W. W. Norton & Company Ltd., 10 Coptic Street, London WC1A 1PU

1 2 3 4 5 6 7 8 9 0

Contents

v

Preface

This score anthology is designed for use in courses that focus on the great masterworks of Western music literature. The selections, which range from Gregorian chant through contemporary music, span a wide variety of forms and genres. Many works are presented in their entirety; others are represented by one or more movements or an excerpt. (In the case of some twentieth-century works, issues of copyright and practicality prevented the inclusion of a complete score.) Operatic excerpts and some choral works are given in piano/vocal scores, while other pieces are in full scores. Translations are provided for all foreign-texted vocal works; in operatic excerpts, these appear in the score as nonliteral singing translations. The anthology is generally arranged chronologically by birthdate of the composer and, within a composer's output, by order of composition.

This collection of scores can serve a variety of teaching needs:

1. as a core anthology or ancillary for a masterworks-oriented music appreciation class, to aid students in improving their listening and music-reading abilities;
2. as a study anthology for a music history course, in which students focus on repertory, genres, and musical styles;
3. as an anthology for an analysis course, providing students with a variety of forms and styles for in-depth study;
4. as a central text for a capstone course in musical styles, in which students learn or review standard repertory through listening and score study;

5. as an ancillary to a beginning conducting course, where the highlighting aids students in following full orchestral scores.

In addition, *The Norton Scores* can function as an independent study tool for students wishing to expand their knowledge of repertory and styles, or as a resource for the instructor teaching any of the courses listed above.

The Norton Scores can be used either independently or with an introductory text. The repertory coordinates with that of *The Enjoyment of Music,* Eighth Edition, by Joseph Machlis and Kristine Forney. Recording packages (eight CDs or cassettes or four CDs or cassettes) accompany this eighth edition of *The Norton Scores.* Also available is a CD-ROM disk (*The Norton CD-ROM Masterworks,* vol. 1), which includes interactive analyses of twelve works chosen from *The Norton Scores,* spanning Gregorian chant through the twentieth century.

A unique system of highlighting is employed in the full scores of this anthology. The highlighting directs those who are just beginning to develop music-reading skills to preselected elements in the score, thus enhancing their listening experience. Students with good music-reading skills will, of course, perceive many additional details. Each system (or group of staves) is covered with a light gray screen, within which the most prominent musical lines are highlighted by white bands. Where two or more simultaneous lines are equally prominent, they are both highlighted. Multiple musical systems on a single page are separated by thin white bands running the full width of the page. (For more information, see "How to Follow the Highlighted Scores" on p. xii.) This highlighting technique has been employed largely for instrumental music; in vocal works, the text serves to guide the less-experienced score reader through the work.

The highlighting is not intended as an analysis of the melodic structure, contrapuntal texture, or any other aspect of the work. In order to follow the most prominent musical line, the highlighting may shift mid-phrase from one instrument or vocal line to another. Since performances differ in interpretation, the highlighting may not always correspond exactly to what is heard in a specific recording. In some twentieth-century works, it is impossible to isolate a single musical line that shows the continuity of the piece. In these works, the listener's attention is directed to the most audible musical events, and the highlighting is kept as simple as possible.

The repertory chosen for this new edition of *The Norton Scores* includes numerous works that reflect important cross-cultural influences from traditional, popular, and non-Western styles. Such mergers of musical styles characterize the following compositions: John Gay's *The Beggar's Opera;* the finale from Haydn's String Quartet, Op. 76, No. 2 (*Quinten*); Chopin's Polonaise in A-flat, Op. 53; the *Habanera* from Bizet's *Carmen;* Joplin's *Maple Leaf Rag;*

Stravinsky's *Petrushka*; Ive's nostalgic song *The Things Our Fathers Loved*; Copland's *Billy the Kid*; and Bernstein's *West Side Story*. Non-Western styles, instruments, and settings occur in the *Rondo alla turca* from Mozart's Piano Sonata in A major, K. 331; Dvořák's Symphony No. 9 (*From the New World*); Tchaikovsky's *The Nutcracker*; Mahler's *Das Lied von der Erde* (*Songs of the Earth*); Debussy's *Prélude à "L'après-midi d'un faune"* (*Prelude to "The Afternoon of a Faun"*); the *Feria* from Ravel's *Rapsodie espagnol (Spanish Rhapsody)*; Ligeti's *Désordre* from *Etudes for Piano*, Book 1; an excerpt from Ung's *Spiral*; and in a Chinese traditional selection, *Er quan ying yue* (*The Moon Reflected on the Second Springs*). Specific information about the multicultural elements of each of these compositions can be found in *The Enjoyment of Music*, Eighth Edition, particularly in the text's Cultural Perspectives.

The role of women in music is prominently reflected in the repertory selected for this edition. Seven pieces by women composers, covering the full chronological gamut, are included: a scene from Hildegard von Bingen's *Ordo virtutum* (*The Play of the Virtues*); a keyboard dance from Elisabeth-Claude Jacquet de la Guerre's *Pièces de Clavecin*; Fanny Mendelssohn Hensel's song *Bergeslust* (*Mountain Yearning*); Clara Schumann's Scherzo, Op. 10, for solo piano; the scherzo from Amy Beach's Violin Sonata in A minor; Lillian Hardin's *Hotter Than That*; and a movement from Libby Larsen's programmatic *Symphony: Water Music*. In addition, several works written expressly for female performers emphasize the important historic role women have played as interpreters of music. These include Monteverdi's *A un giro sol*, possibly written for the famous Concerto delle donne (Singing Ladies of Ferrara); Mozart's Piano Concerto in G major, K. 453, written for his student Barbara Ployer; and Crumb's *Ancient Voices of Children*, premiered by the phenomenal vocalist Jan DeGaetani.

I should like to thank a number of people for assistance in preparing this edition of *The Norton Scores:* Jeanne Scheppach, who has been an invaluable research assistant for this edition; Martha Graedel and Anne White, both of W. W. Norton, who ably collected the scores and handled the permissions; David Hamilton, who once again has expertly guided the coordination of the recordings with *The Norton Scores*; Michael Ochs, who has very capably supervised all production aspects of the scores; and Susan Gaustad, who has meticulously copyedited this edition and has served as project editor at W. W. Norton. I am deeply indebted to them all.

How to Follow the Highlighted Scores

By following the highlighted bands throughout a work, the listener will be able to read the score and recognize the most important or most audible musical lines. The following principles are illustrated on the facing page in an excerpt from Beethoven's Symphony No. 5 in C minor (first movement).

1. The musical line that is most prominent at any time is highlighted by a white band shown against light gray screening.
2. When a highlighted line continues from one system (group of staves) or page to the next, the white band ends with an arrow head (>) that indicates the continuation of the highlighted line, which begins on the next system with an indented arrow shape.
3. Multiple systems (more than one on a page) are separated by narrow white bands across the full width of the page. Watch carefully for these bands so that you do not overlook a portion of the score.
4. At times, two musical lines are highlighted simultaneously, indicating that they are equally audible. On first listening, it may be best to follow only one of these.
5. When more than one instrument plays the same musical line, in unison or octaves (called doubling), the instrument whose line is most audible is highlighted.
6. CD track numbers are given throughout the scores at the beginning of each movement and at important structural points within movements. They appear in a ☐ for the 8-CD set and in a ◇ for the 4-CD set, where appropriate.

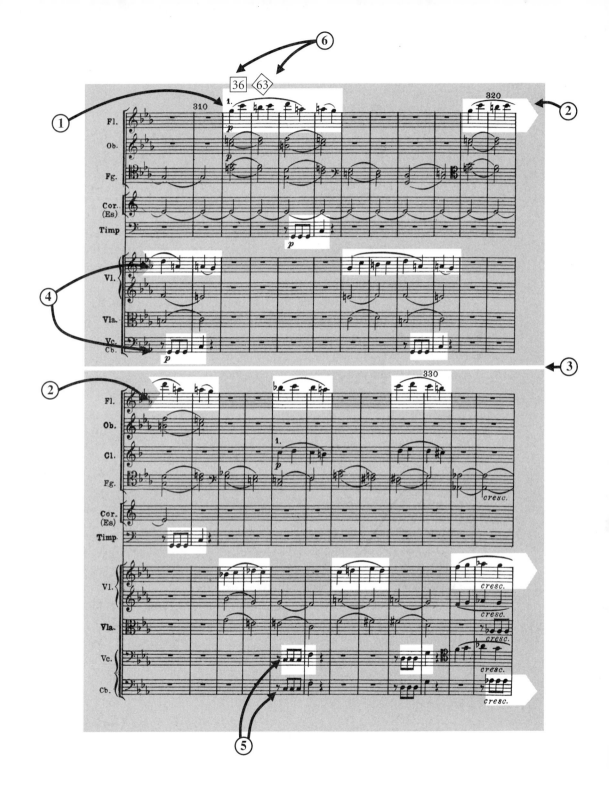

A Note on the Recordings

Sets of recordings of the works in *The Norton Scores* are available from the publisher. There are five sets in all: an eight-cassette or eight-CD set that includes all the works in the two volumes of the anthology; a four-cassette or four-CD set that includes selected works from both volumes; and a CD-ROM disk (entitled *MasterWorks*) that includes twelve of the works selected from the two volumes, with interactive analyses. The location of each work in the various recording packages is noted in the score to the right of the title.

Example (for Schubert's *Erlkönig*):

8CD: 5/ 1 – 8
4CD: 3/ 6 – 13
8Cas: 5A/1
4Cas: 3A/2
MasterWorks

   8 CD or 4 CD: after the colon, a number designates the individual CD within the set; after a diagonal slash, a boxed number gives the track or tracks on that CD devoted to the work.

   8 Cas or 4 Cas: after the colon, a number designates the individual cassette within the set and a letter indicates side A or B of the cassette; after a diagonal slash, a numeral gives the selection number(s) on that cassette side.

   For an overview of which works appear on the various recording sets, see Appendix D.

1. Franz Schubert

Erlkönig (Erlking), D. 328
(1815)

8CD: 5/ 1 – 8
4CD: 3/ 6 – 13
8Cas: 5A/1
4Cas: 3A/2
MasterWorks

Editor's note: In performance, this Lied is often transposed to F minor, and occasionally to E minor.

TEXT AND TRANSLATION

Wer reitet so spät durch Nacht und Wind?
Es ist der Vater mit seinem Kind;
er hat den Knaben wohl in dem Arm,
er fasst ihn sicher, er hält ihn warm.

"Mein Sohn, was birgst du so bang dein Gesicht?"
"Siehst, Vater, du den Erlkönig nicht?
den Erlenkönig mit Kron' und Schweif?"
"Mein Sohn, es ist ein Nebelstreif."

"Du liebes Kind, komm, geh mit mir!
gar schöne Spiele spiel' ich mit dir;
manch' bunte Blumen sind an dem Strand;

meine Mutter hat manch' gülden Gewand."

"Mein Vater, mein Vater, und hörest du nicht,
was Erlenkönig mir leise verspricht?"
"Sei ruhig, bleibe ruhig, mein Kind;
in dürren Blättern säuselt der Wind."

"Willst, feiner Knabe, du mit mir geh'n?
meine Töchter sollen dich warten schön;
meine Töchter führen den nächtlichen Reih'n
und wiegen und tanzen und singen dich ein."

"Mein Vater, mein Vater, und siehst du nicht
    dort,
Erlkönigs Töchter am düstern
    Ort?"
"Mein Sohn, mein Sohn, ich seh' es genau,
es scheinen die alten Weiden so grau."

"Ich liebe dich, mich reizt deine schöne Gestalt,
und bist du nicht willig, so brauch' ich Gewalt."
"Mein Vater, mein Vater, jetzt fasst er mich an!
Erlkönig hat mir ein Leids gethan!"

Dem Vater grauset's, er reitet geschwind,
er hält in Armen das ächzende Kind,
erreicht den Hof mit Müh und
    Noth:
in seinem Armen das Kind war todt.

Who rides so late through night and wind?
It is a father with his child:
he has the boy close in his arm,
he holds him tight, he keeps him warm.

"My son, why do you hide your face in fear?"
"Father, don't you see the Erlking?
The Erlking with his crown and train?"
"My son, it is a streak of mist."

"You dear child, come with me!
I'll play very lovely games with you.
There are lots of colorful flowers by the
    shore;
my mother has some golden robes."

"My father, my father, and don't you hear
the Erlking whispering promises to me?"
"Be still, stay calm, my child;
it's the wind rustling in the dry leaves."

"My fine lad, do you want to come with me?
My daughters will take care of you;
my daughters lead off the nightly dance,
and they'll rock and dance and sing you to
    sleep."

"My father, my father, and don't you
    see
the Erlking's daughters over there in the
    shadows?"
"My son, my son, I see it clearly,
it's the gray sheen of the old willows."

"I love you, your beautiful form delights me!
And if you are not willing, then I'll use force."
"My father, my father, now he's grasping me!
The Erlking has hurt me!"

The father shudders, he rides swiftly,
he holds the moaning child in his arms;
with effort and urgency he reaches the
    courtyard:
in his arms the child was dead.

JOHANN WOLFGANG VON GOETHE

2. Franz Schubert

Die Forelle (The Trout) (1817)

8CD: 5/ 9 – 11

8Cas: 5A/2

TEXT AND TRANSLATION

In einem Bächlein helle,	In a bright little stream
Da schoss in froher Eil'	the good-natured trout
Die launische Forelle	darted about in joyous haste
Vorüber wie ein Pfeil.	like an arrow.
Ich stand an dem Gestade	I stood on the bank
Und sah in süsser Ruh'	and watched in sweet repose
Des muntern Fischleins Bade	the bath of the lively little fish
Im klaren Bächlein zu.	in the clear water.
[last two lines repeated]	
Ein Fischer mit der Rute	A fisherman with his rod
Wohl an dem Ufer stand,	also stood on the bank
Und sah's mit kaltem Blute,	and cold-bloodedly watched
Wie sich das Fischlein wand.	the little fish swimming to and fro.
So lang' dem Wasser Helle,	As long as the water stays clear,
So dacht, ich, nicht gebricht,	I thought, he won't
So fängt er die Forelle	catch the trout
Mit seiner Angel nicht.	with his rod.
[last two lines repeated]	
Doch endlich ward dem Diebe	Bur finally the wait grew too long
Die zeit zu lang. Er macht	for the thief. He made
Das Bächlein tückisch trübe,	the brook all muddy,
Und eh' ich es gedacht,	and before I knew it,
So zuckte seine Rute,	his rod quivered,
Das Fischlein zappelt dran,	the little fish wriggled at its end,
Und ich mit regem Blute	and I, my blood boiling,
Sah die Betrog'ne an.	gazed at the betrayed one.
[two last lines repeated]	

C. F. SCHUBART

3. Franz Schubert

Piano Quintet in A major
(the *Trout*), Fourth Movement
(1819)

8CD: 5/ 12 – 18
8Cas: 5A/3

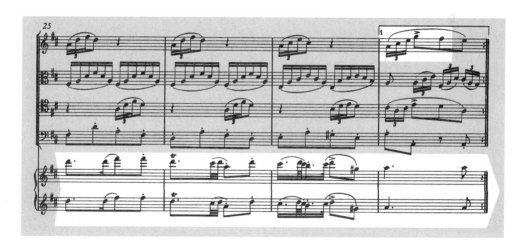

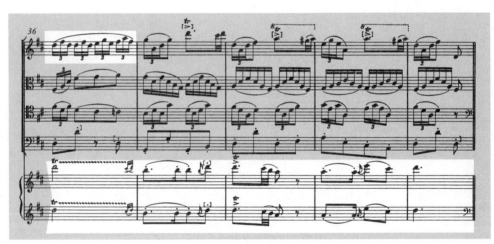

14

Var. II

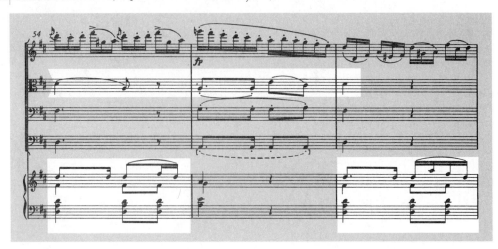

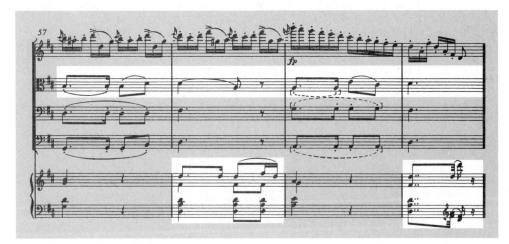

15

Var. III

16

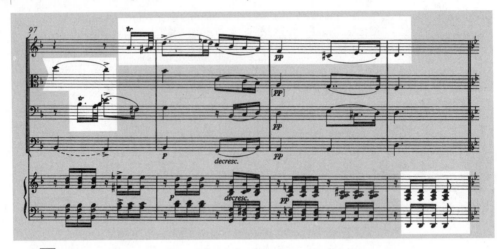

17

Var. V 101

4. Hector Berlioz

Symphonie fantastique,
Fourth and Fifth Movements (1830)

8CD: 5/ 31 – 43
4CD: 3/ 30 – 35
8Cas: 5B/1–2
4Cas: 3B/1

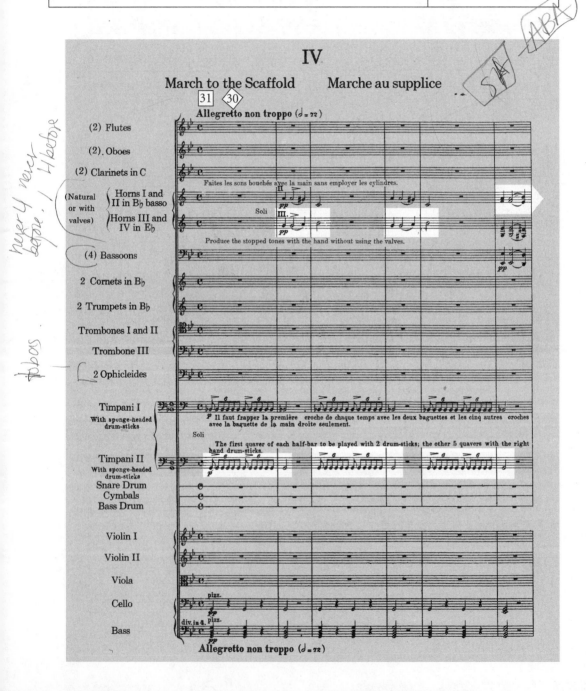

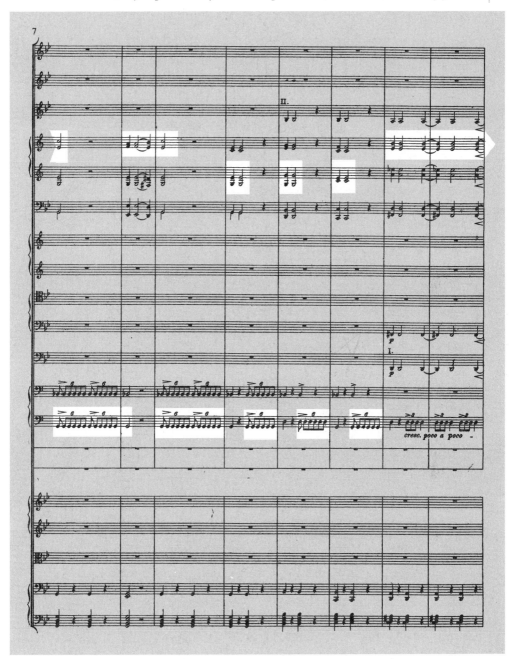

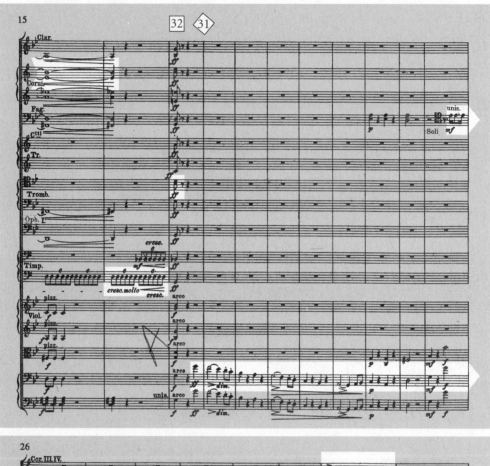

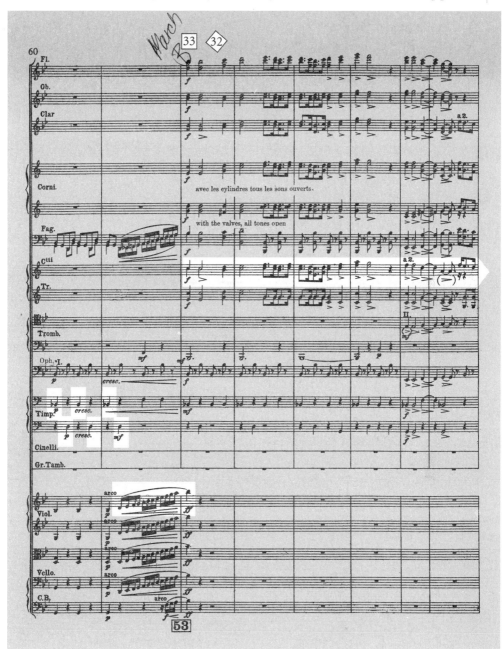

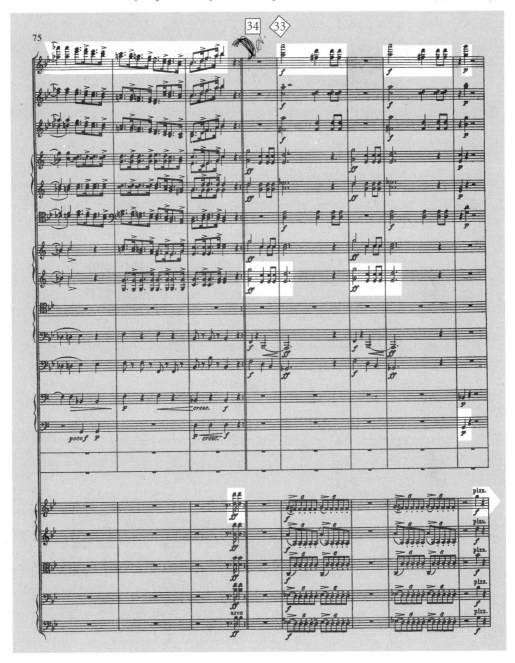

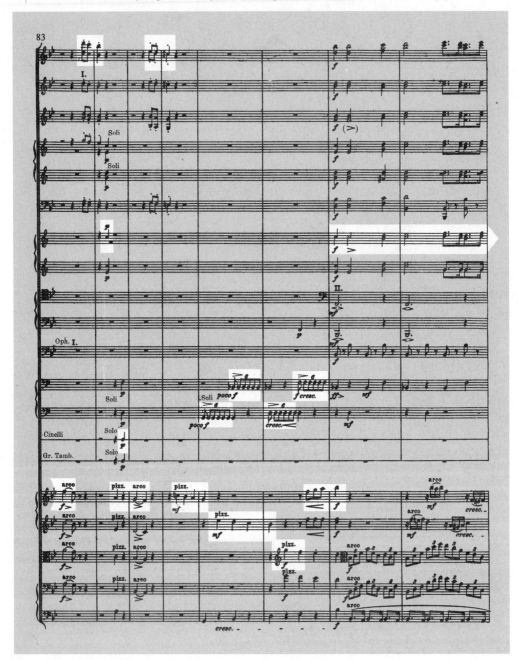

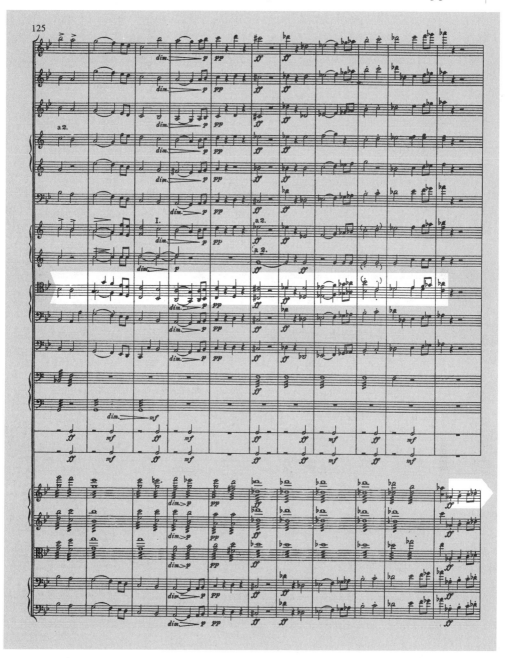

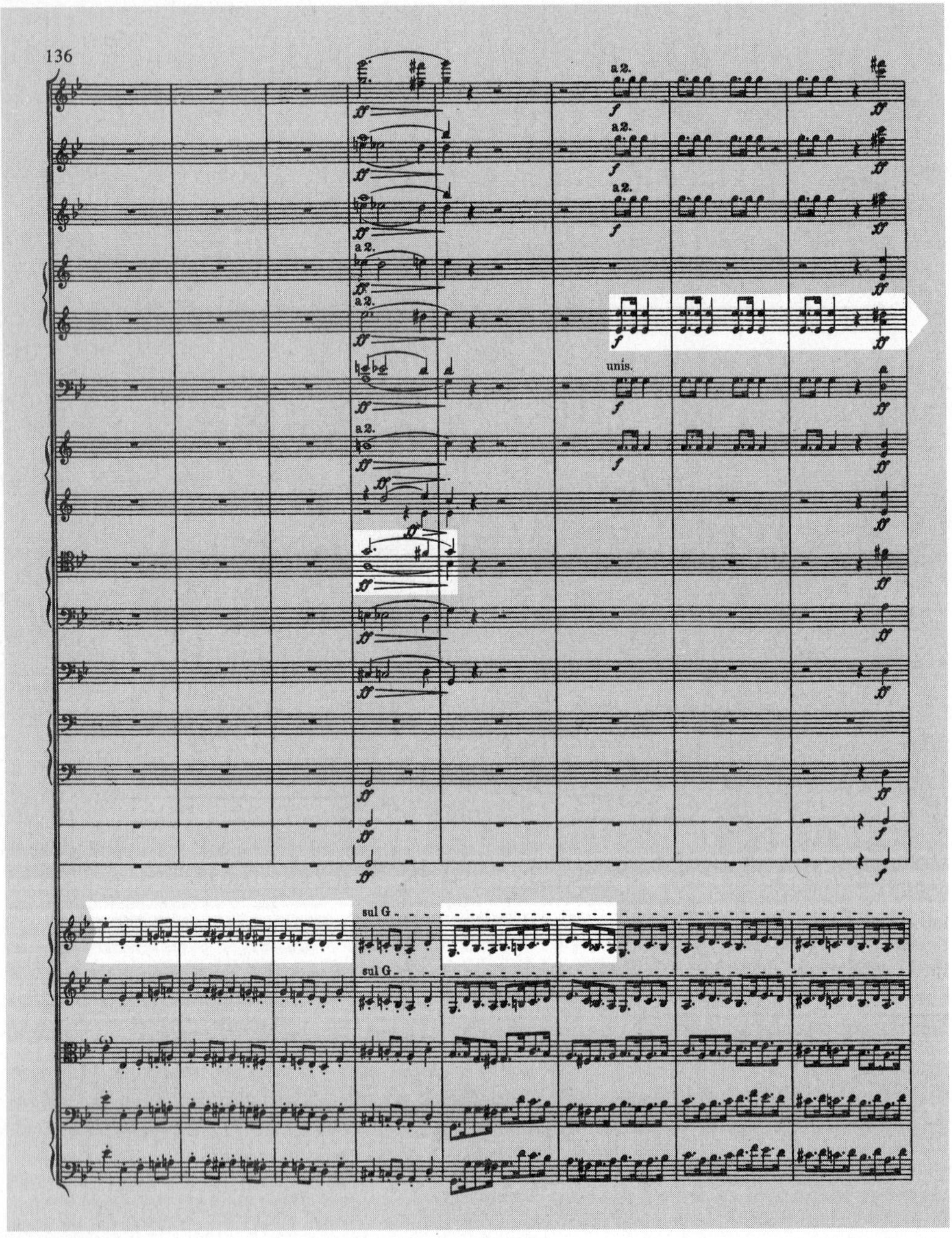
136
a 2.
unis.
sul G

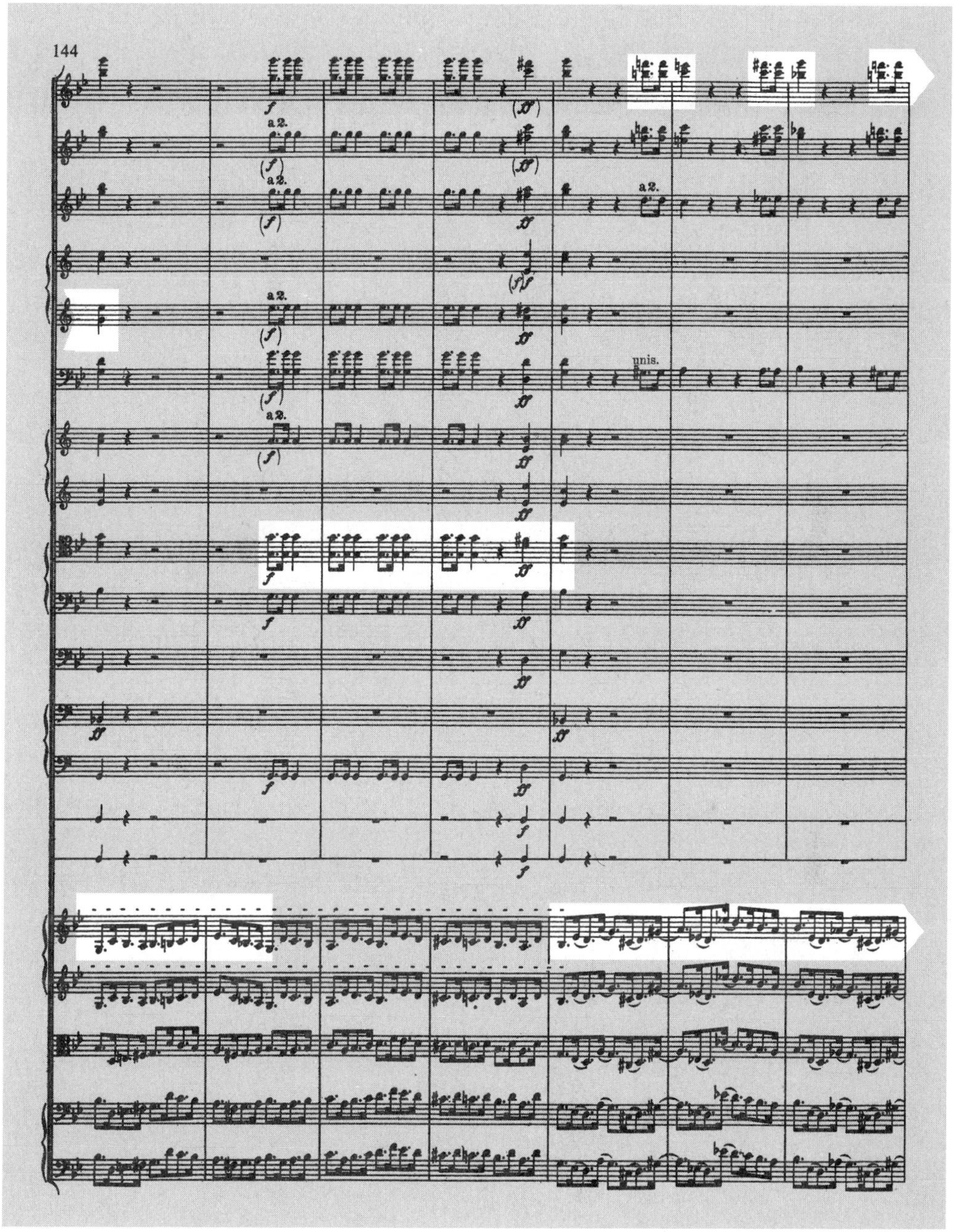
144
a2.
unis.

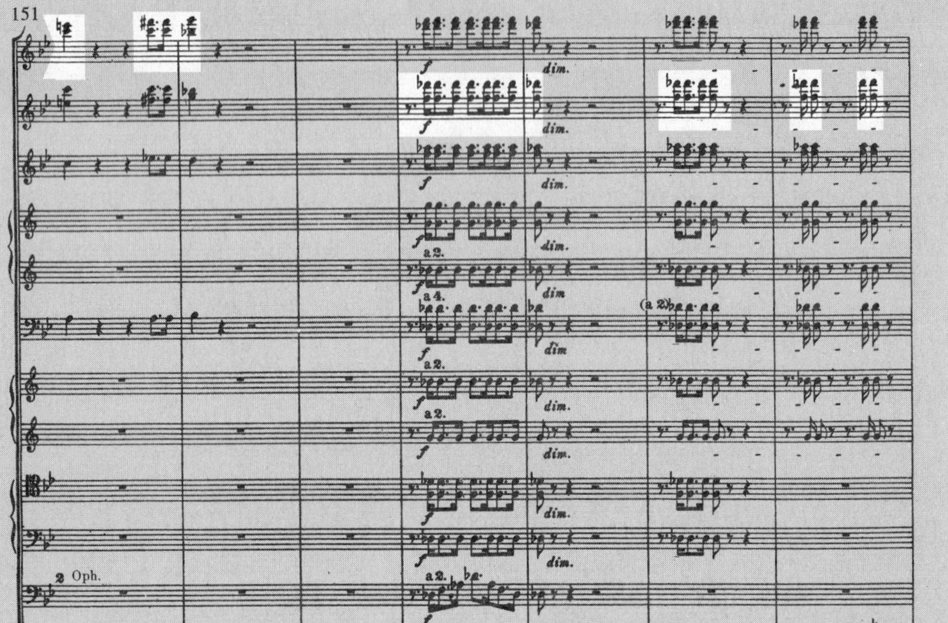
151
a 2.
a 4.
(a 2)
2 Oph.
muta in B♮
dim.
f
mf
ff

158
a2.
36
35
I. Solo
pp dolce assai ed appassionato
Trois Timbaliers
Three drummers

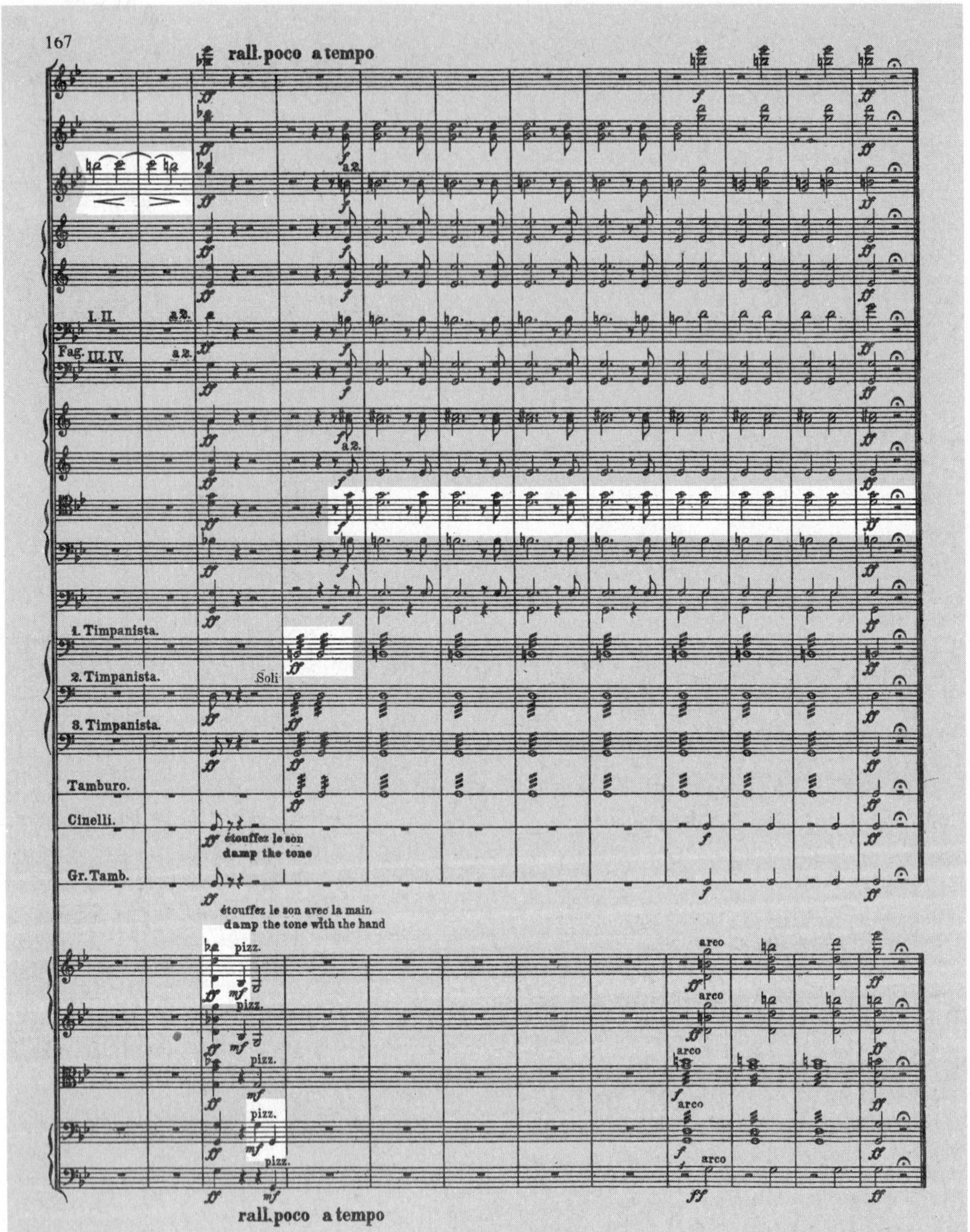
167
rall. poco a tempo
a 2.
I. II.
Fag.
III. IV.
1. Timpanista.
2. Timpanista.
Soli
3. Timpanista.
Tamburo.
Cinelli.
étouffez le son
damp the tone
Gr. Tamb.
étouffez le son avec la main
damp the tone with the hand
pizz.
arco
rall. poco a tempo

V

Dream of a Witches' Sabbath   Songe d'une nuit du sabbat

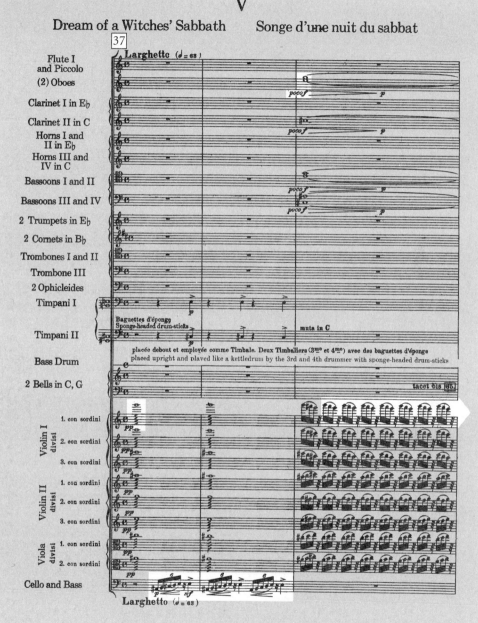

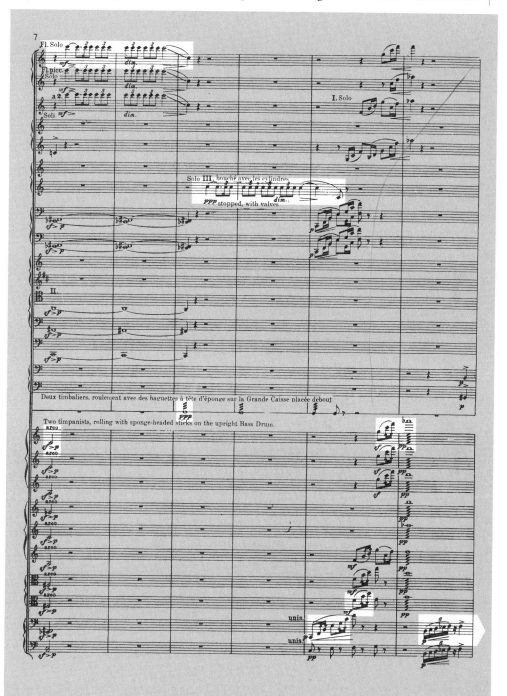

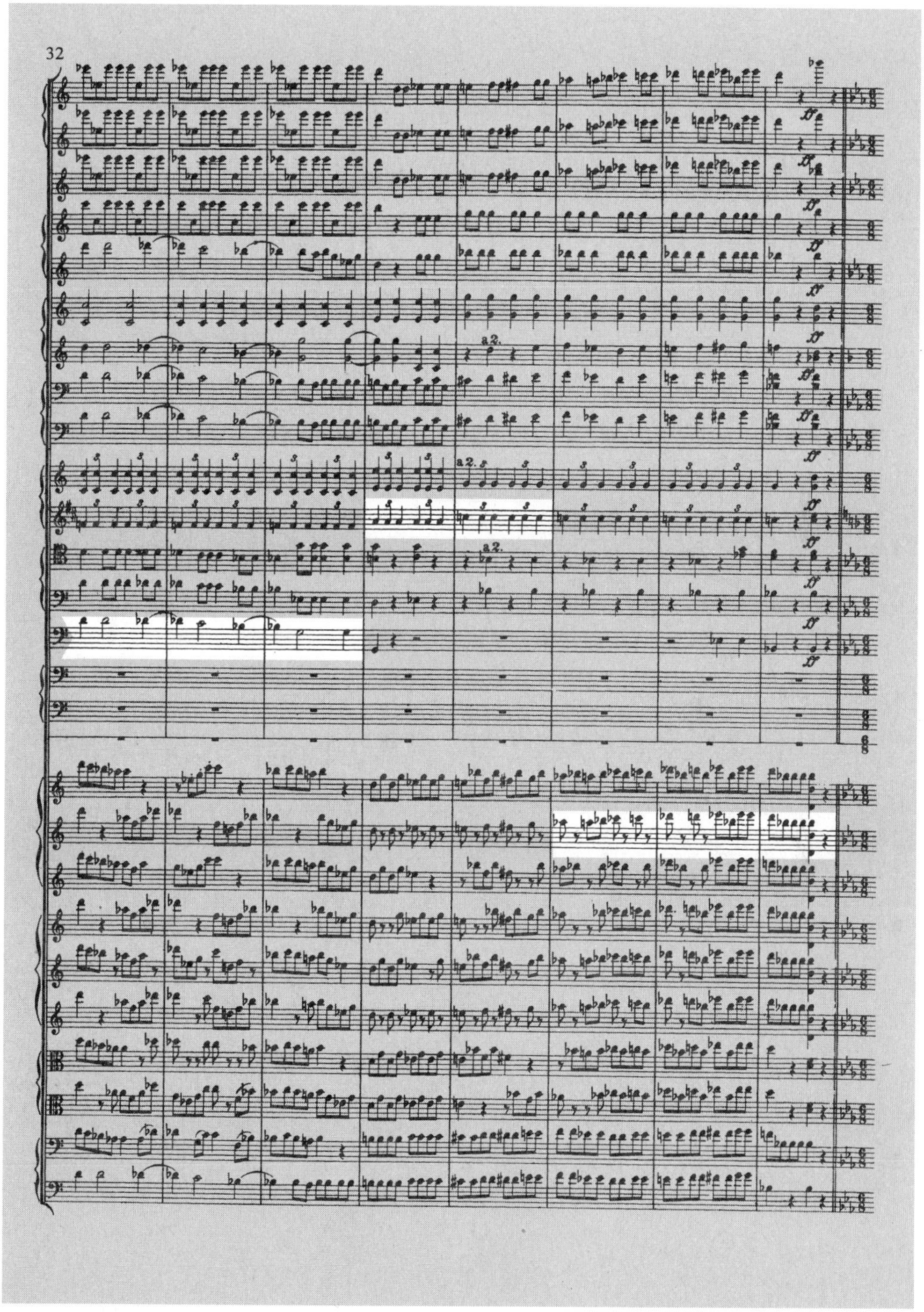
32
a2.
a2.
a2.

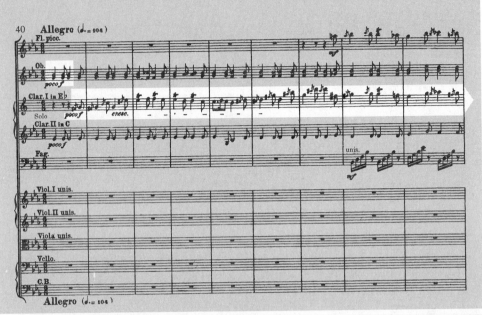

67
Fl.
Fl. picc.
Ob.
Clar.
a 2.
Cor.
a 2.
unis.
Fag.
Tr.
Ctti
Tromb.
Oph.
Timp.
Viol.

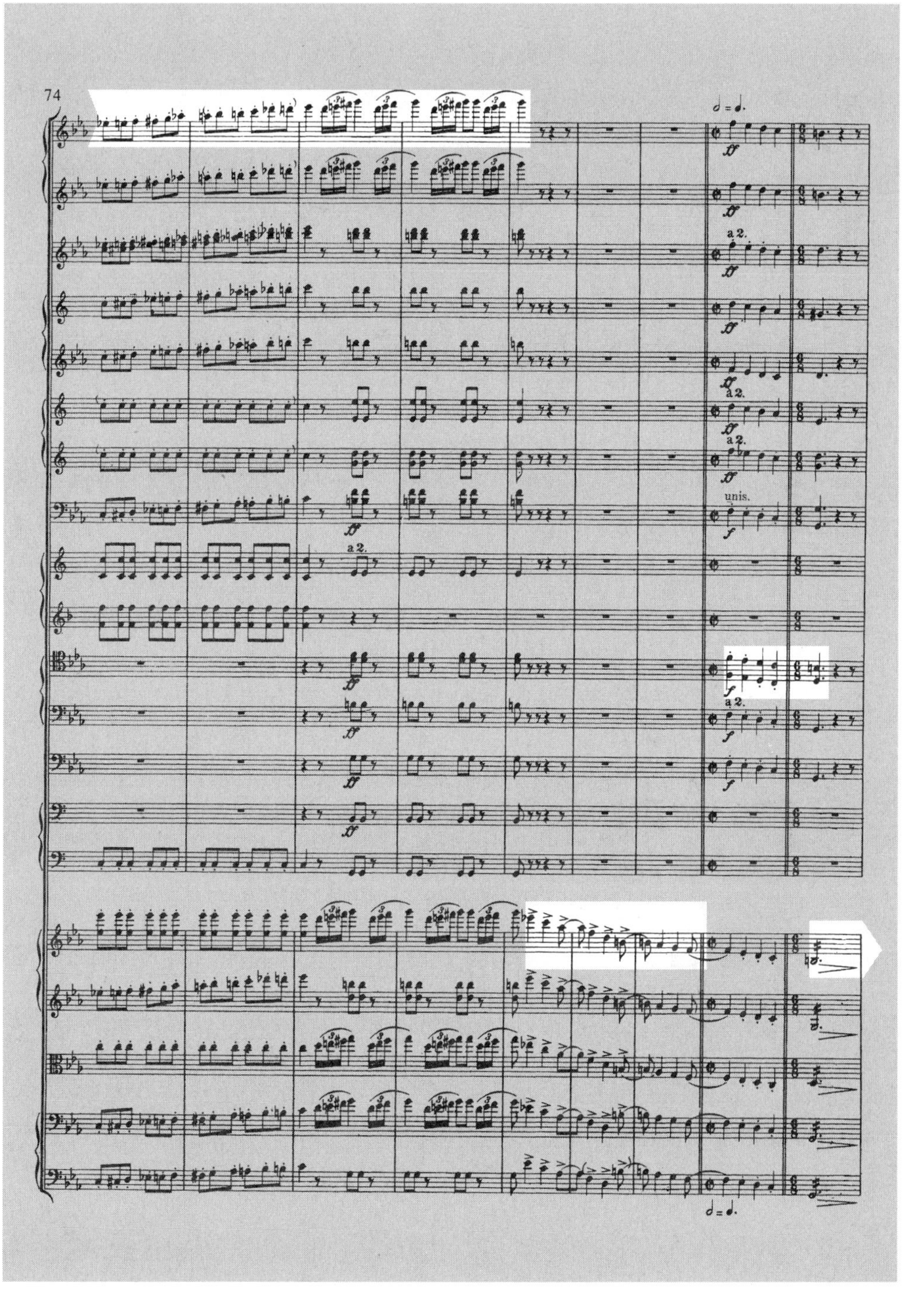
74
a 2.
unis.

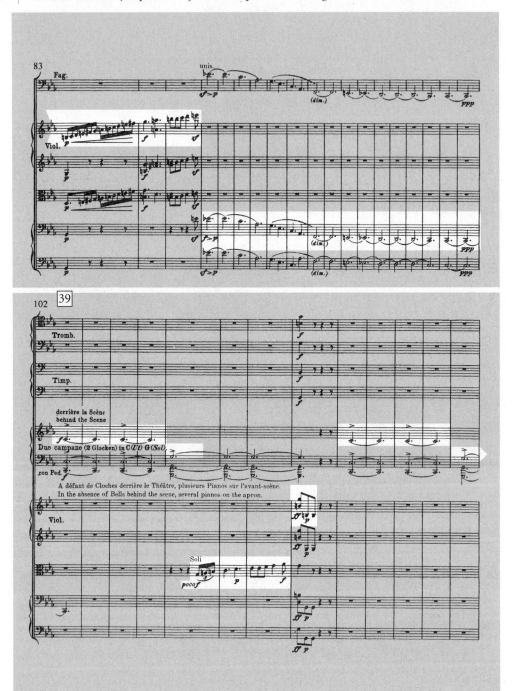

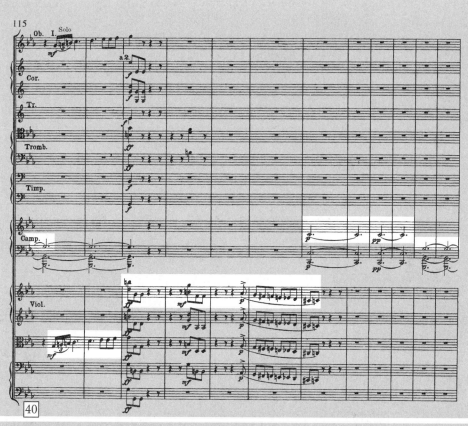

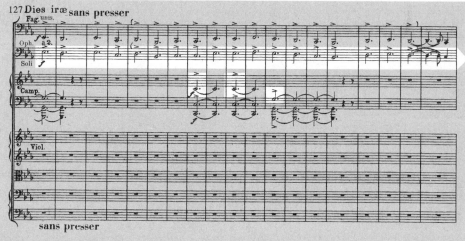

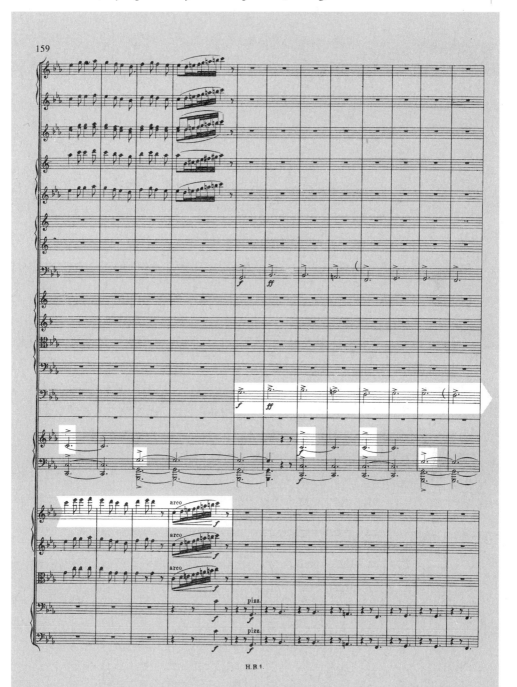

H.B.1.

171

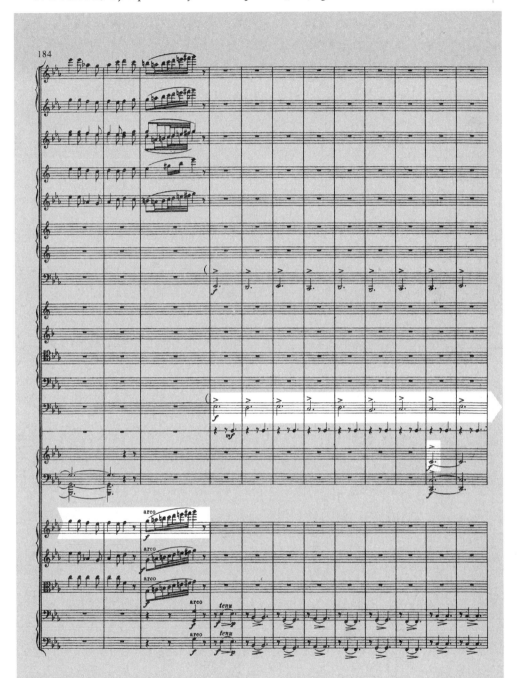

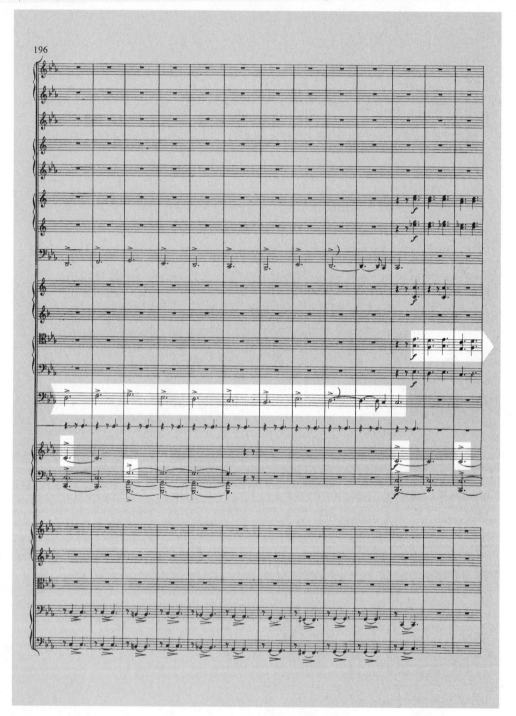

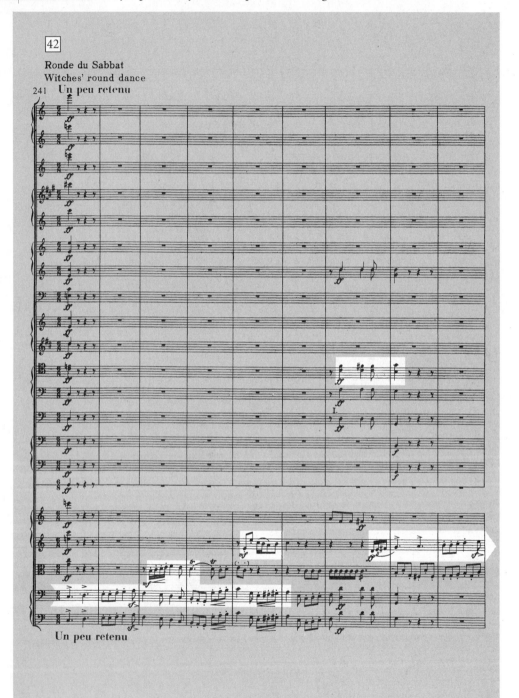

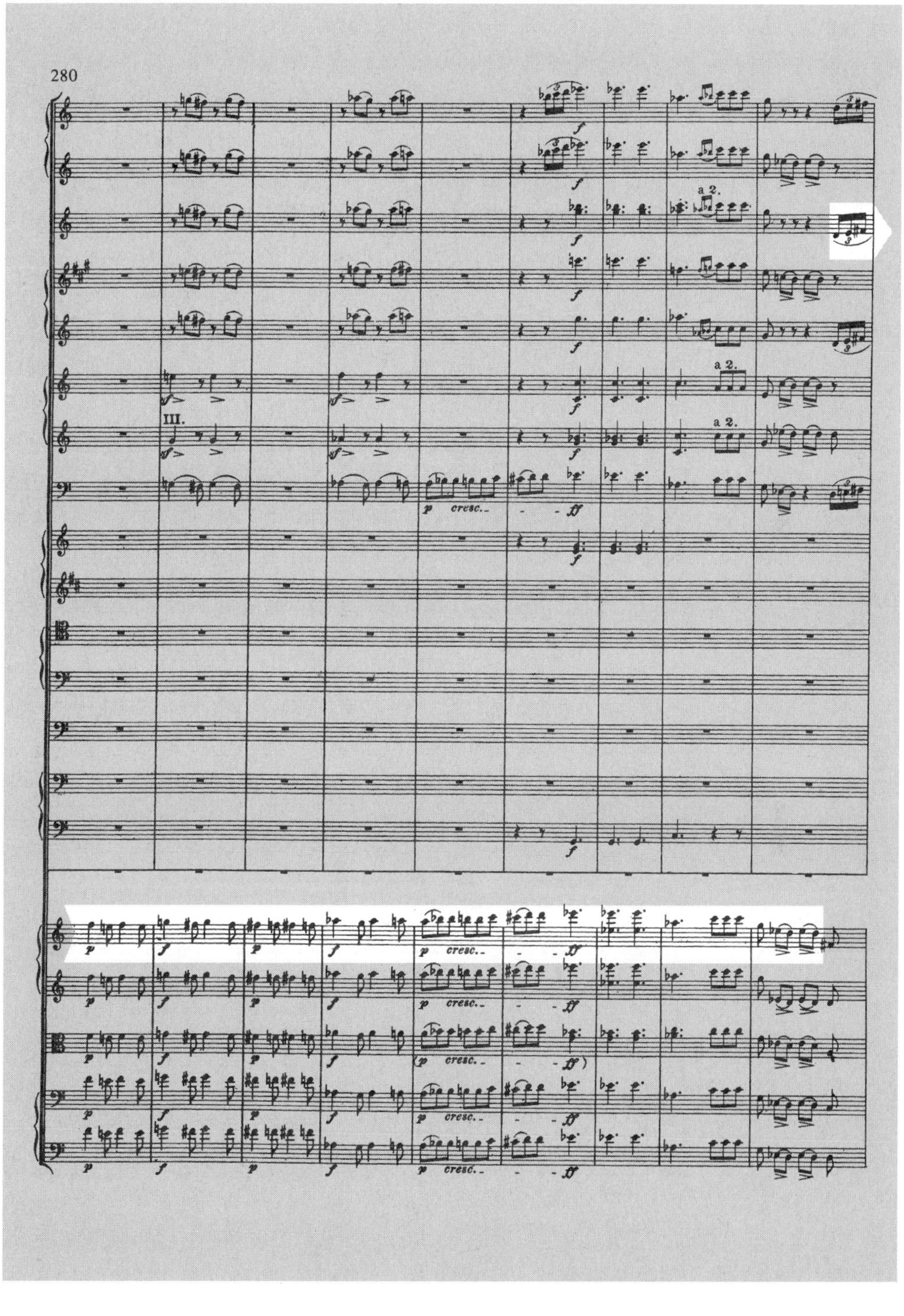
280
a 2.
III.
cresc.

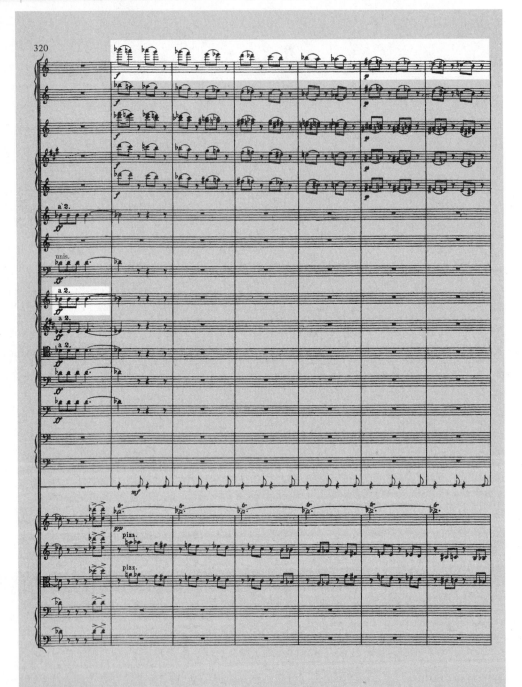

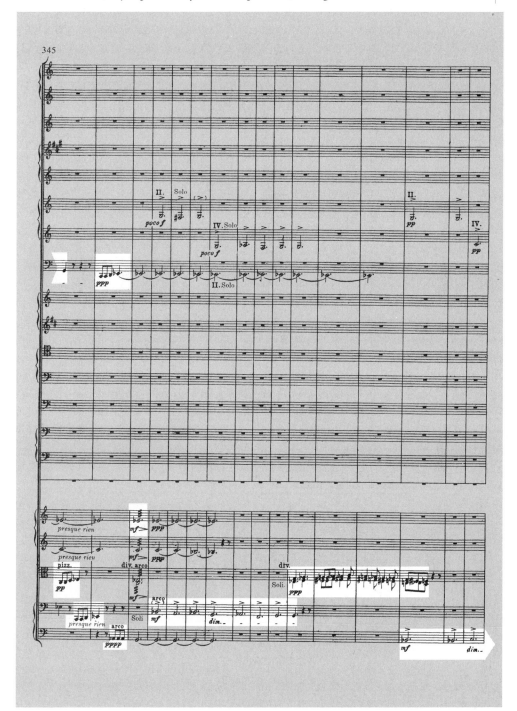

371
bouché avec les cylindres
II.
poco sf > p
Les deux Timbaliers réunis
Both drummers together
p cresc. poco a poco
p
p
cresc. poco a poco
poco a poco
poco a poco

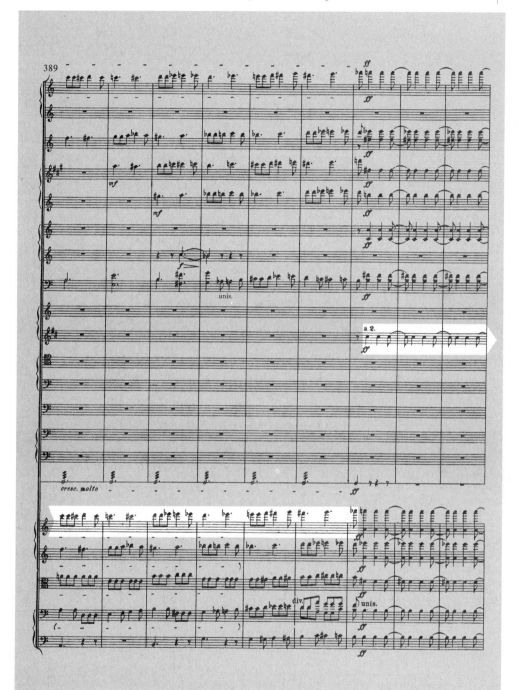

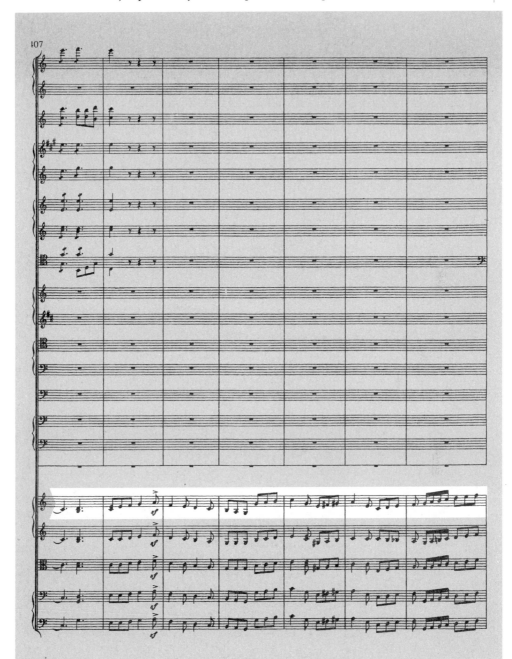

43
Dies irae et Ronde du Sabbat ensemble
414 Dies irae and witches' round dance together

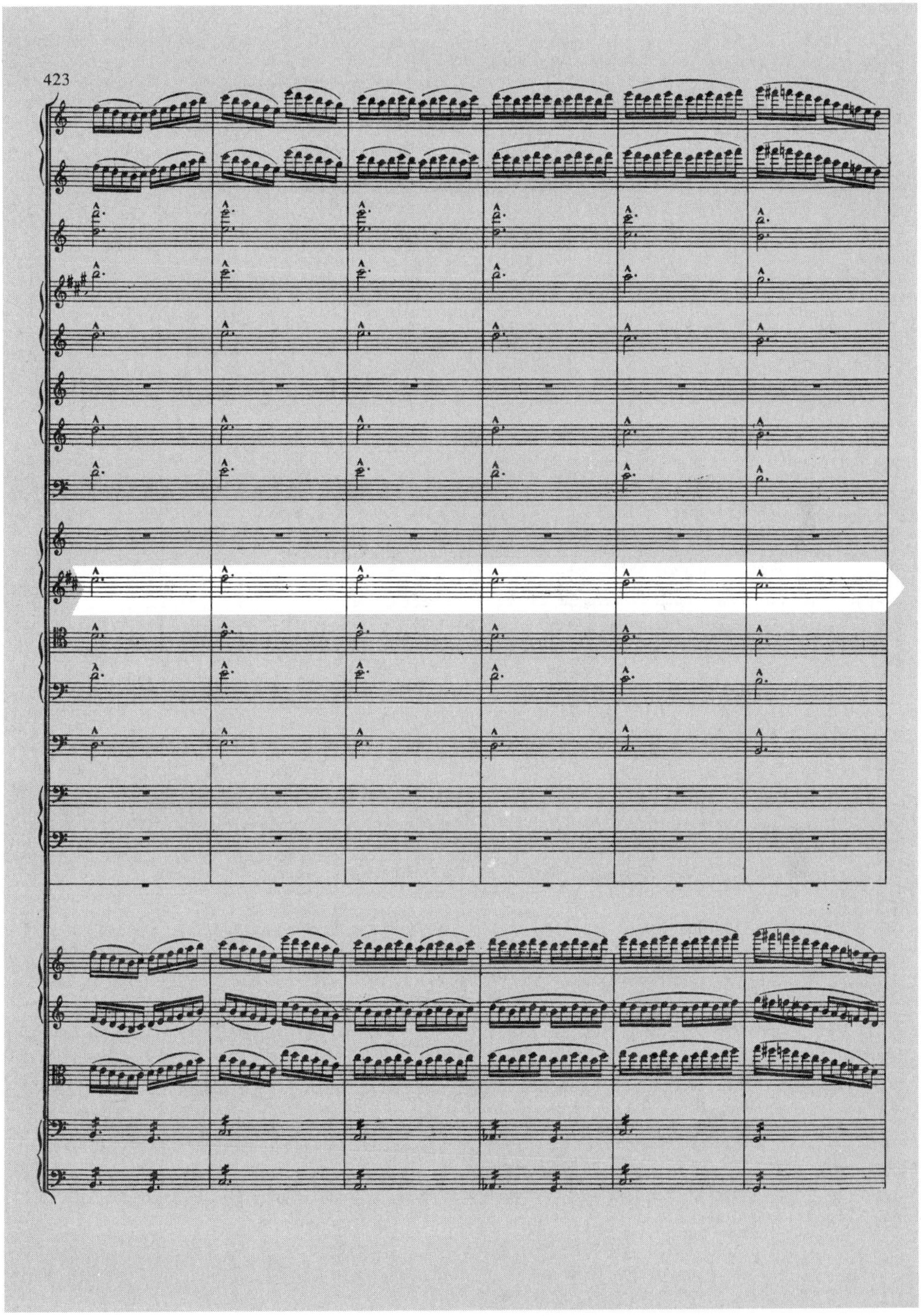
423

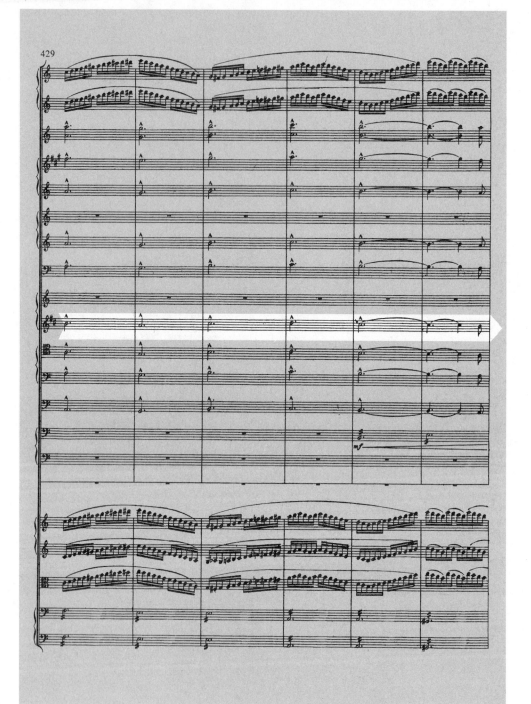

435

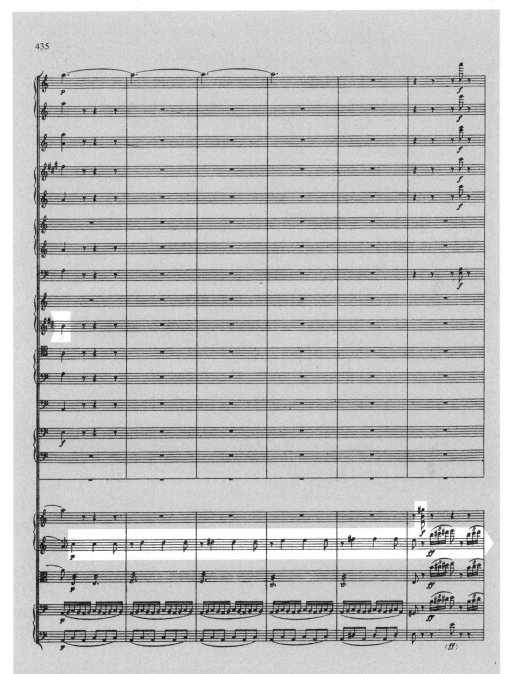

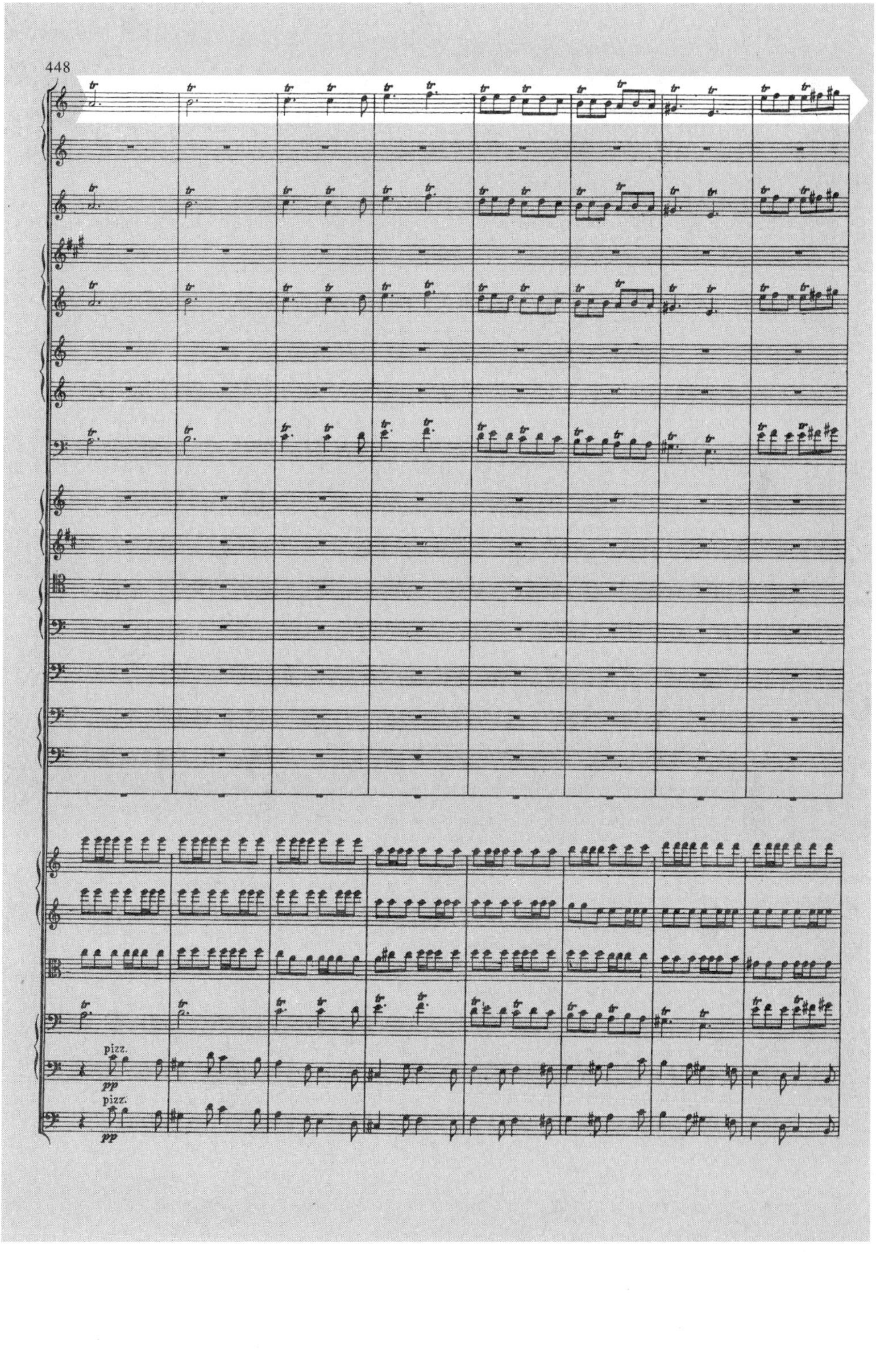
448
tr
pizz.
pp

456
Soli
p légèrement
I.
p légèrement
p légèrement
I.
p légèrement
arco

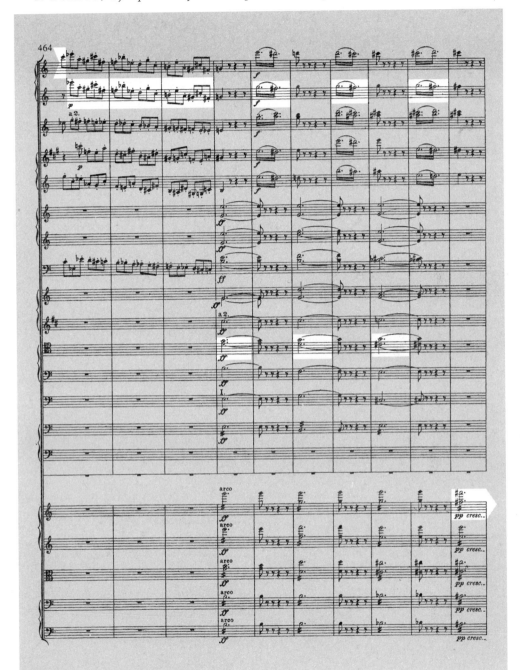

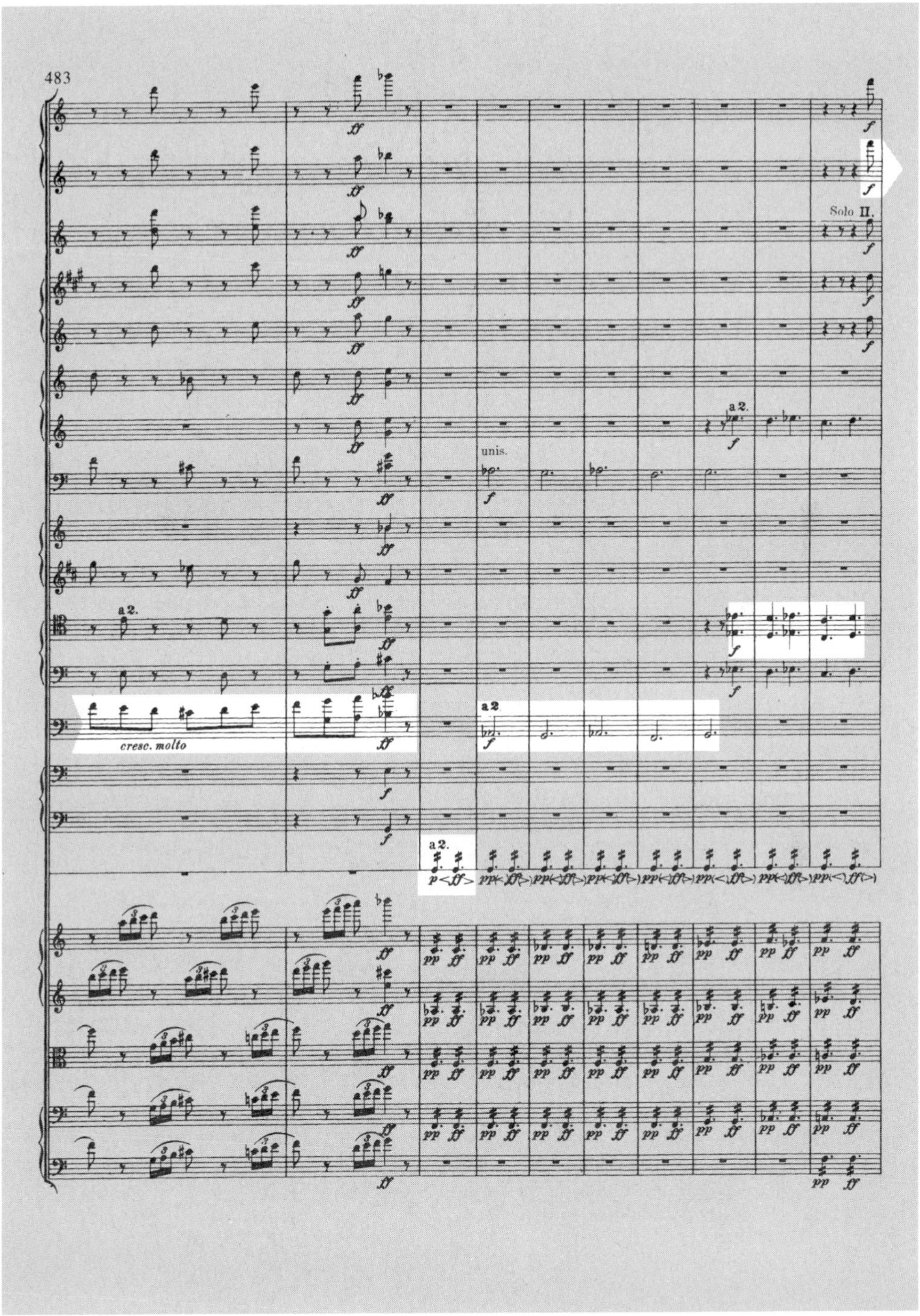
483
Solo II.
a 2.
unis.
a 2.
a 2
cresc. molto
a 2.

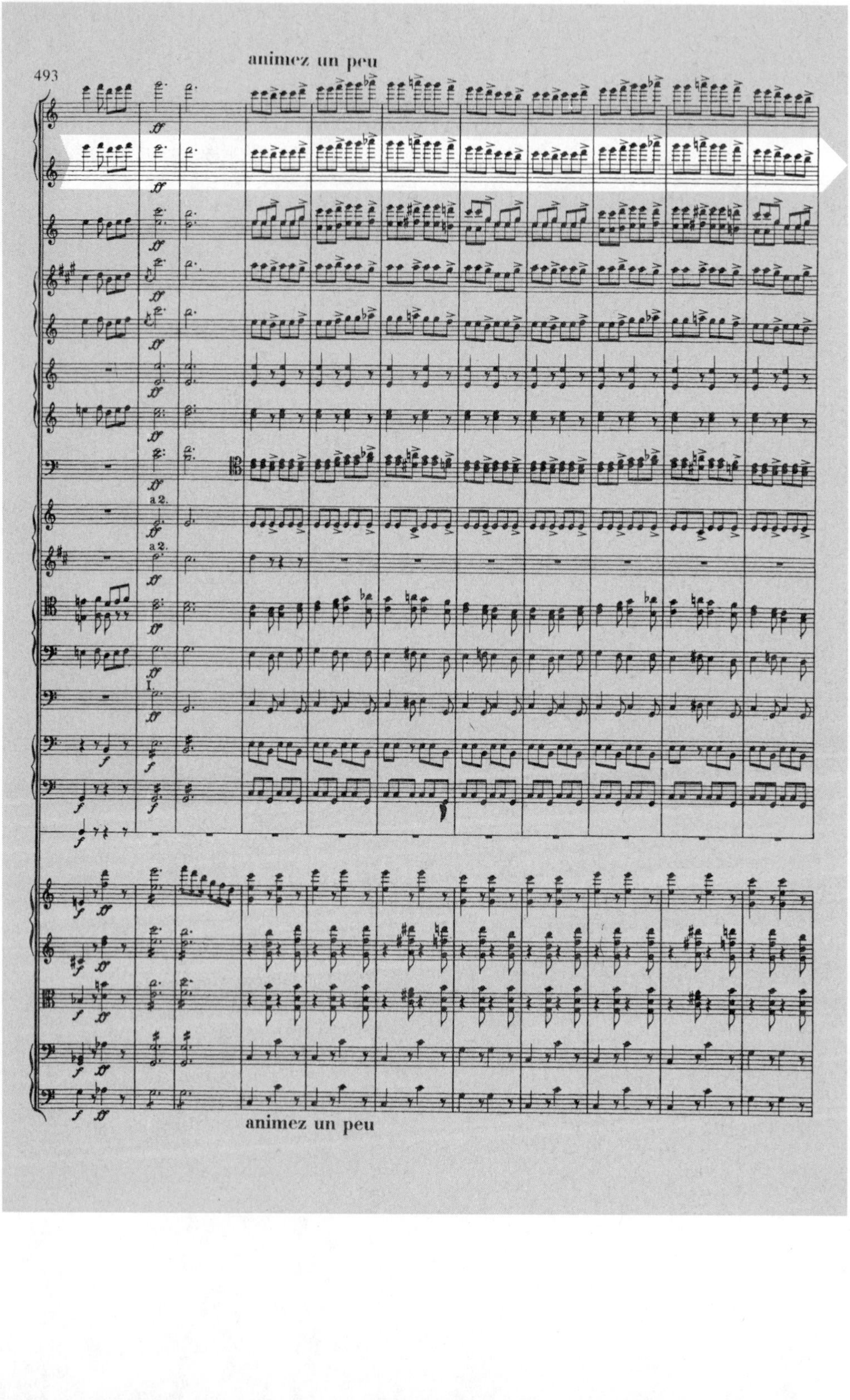
animez un peu
493
a 2.
a 2.
I.
animez un peu

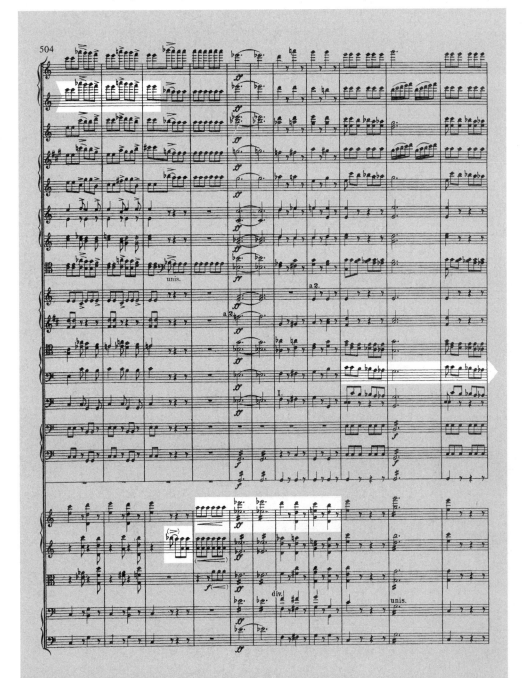

515
tenu
unis.
Coup frappé sur une Cymbale avec une baguette couverte d'éponge ou un tampon
Struck on a cymbal with a sponge-headed drum-stick or a padded stick
Cinelli.

5. Fanny Mendelssohn Hensel

Bergeslust (Mountain Yearning), Op. 10, No. 5
(1847)

8CD: 5/ 19 – 21
8Cas: 5A/4

homophonic

19

Allegro molto vivace e leggiero

O

Lust, vom Berg zu schau - en weit ü - ber Wald und Strom,

hoch ü - ber sich__ den blau - en, den kla - ren Him - mels - dom, hoch

Wind; _____ Ge - dan - ken ü - ber-

flie - gen die Vö - gel und den

Wind, die Vö - gel und den Wind. _____

[21]

_____ Die

Wol - ken ziehn her - nie - - der, das Vög - lein senkt sich gleich, Ge -

dan - ken gehn und Lie - - der bis in das Him - mel - reich, Ge -

dan - ken gehn, Ge - dan - - - - - - - - - - - - ken bis in das Him - mel -

reich. Ge - dan - ken gehn und Lie - - der

TEXT AND TRANSLATION

O Lust, vom Berg zu schauen
Weit über Wald und Strom,
Hoch über sich den blauen,
den klaren Himmelsdom.

What longing to gaze from the mountaintop
far across forest and stream,
with, high above, the blue,
clear dome of heaven.

Vom Berge Vögel fliegen,
Und Wolken so geschwind,
Gedanken überfliegen
Die Vögel und den Wind.

From the mountain, birds fly
and clouds speed away,
thoughts soar over
the birds and the wind.

Die Wolken zieh'n hernieder,
Das Vöglein senkt sich gleich,
Gedanken geh'n und Lieder
Bis in das Himmelreich

The clouds drift downward,
the little bird will soon alight,
but thoughts and songs
reach to the realm of heaven.

JOSEPH FREIHERR VON EICHENDORFF

6. Felix Mendelssohn

Violin Concerto in E minor, Op. 64,
First Movement (1844)

8CD: 5/ 22 – 30
8Cas: 5A/5

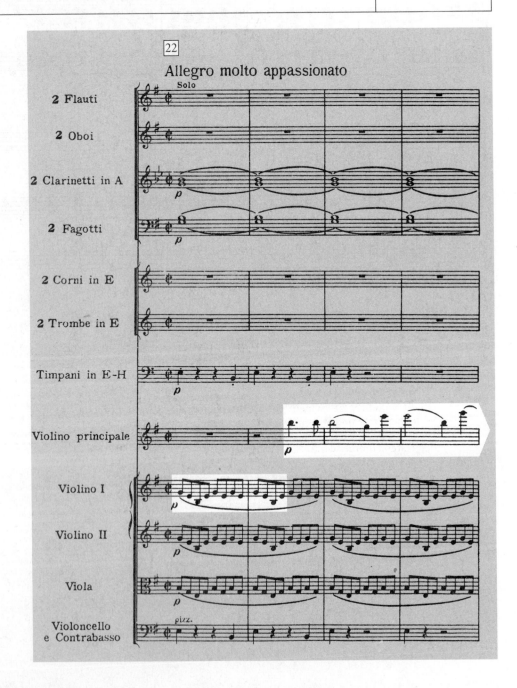

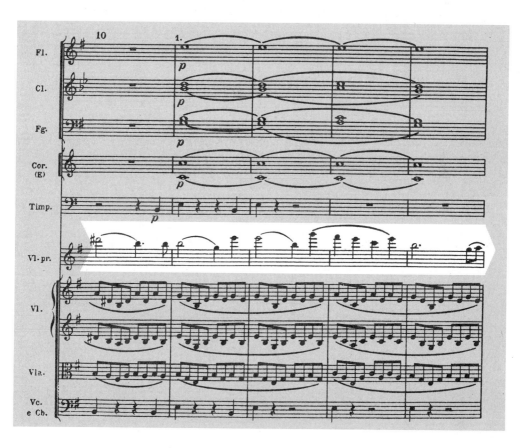

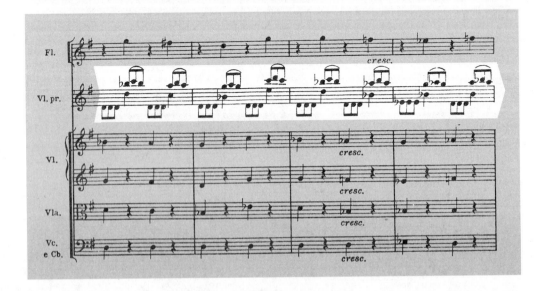

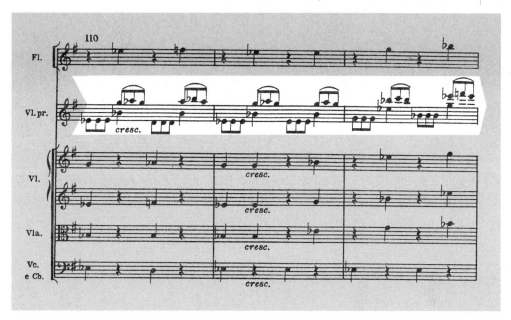

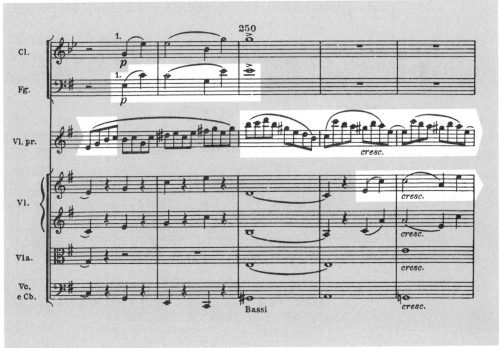

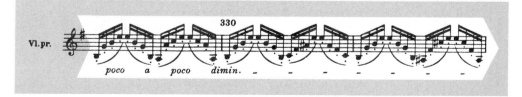

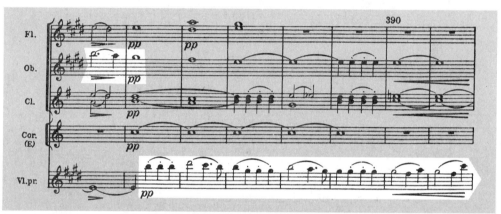

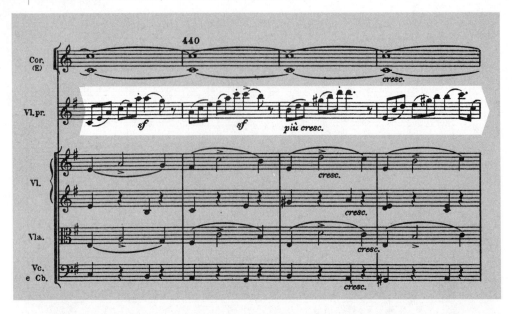

7. Frédéric François Chopin

Prelude in E minor, Op. 28, No. 4
(published 1839)

8CD: 5/ 48 – 49
8Cas: 5A/7

8. Chopin

Polonaise in A-flat major, Op. 53
(1842)

8CD: 5/ 44 – 47

4CD: 3/ ⟨18⟩ – ⟨21⟩

8Cas: 5A/6

4Cas: 3A/4

MasterWorks

9. Robert Schumann

"Und wüssten's die Blumen"
("And if the flowers knew"),
from *Dichterliebe (A Poet's Love)*,
No. 8 (1840)

8CD: 5/ 50 – 53
4CD: 3/ 14 – 17
8Cas: 5A/8
4Cas: 3A/3

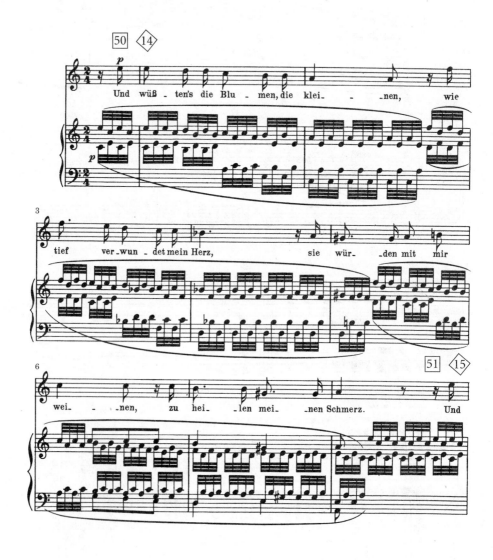

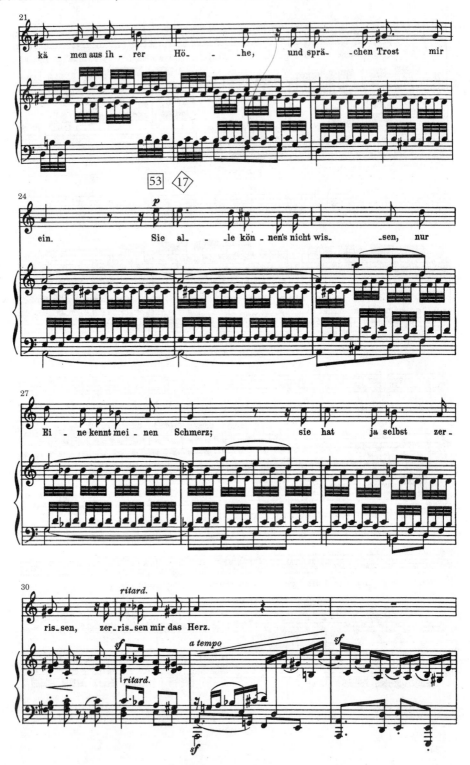

TEXT AND TRANSLATION

Und wüssten's die Blumen, die kleinen,	And if the flowers, the little ones, knew
Wie tief verwundet mein Herz,	how deeply my heart is wounded,
Sie würden mit mir weinen,	they would weep with me
Zu heilen meinen Schmerz.	to heal my pain.
Und wüssten's die Nachtigallen,	And if the nightingales knew
Wie ich so traurig und krank,	how sad and sick I am,
Sie liessen fröhlich erschallen	they would happily sound out
Erquickenden Gesang.	their life-affirming song.
Und wüssten sie mein Wehe,	And if the little golden stars
Die goldenen Sternelein,	knew my hurt,
Sie kämen aus ihrer Höhe,	they would descend from their heights
Und sprächen Trost mir ein.	and speak words of comfort to me.
Sie alle können's nicht wissen,	All of these cannot know,
Nur Eine kennt meinen Schmerz;	only one understands my pain;
Sie hat ja selbst zerrissen,	because she herself has torn—
Zerrissen mir das Herz.	has torn my heart in two.

HEINRICH HEINE

10. Franz Liszt

La campanella (The Little Bell), from
Transcendental Etudes after Paganini, No. 3
(1838–39; rev. 1851)

violinist.

8CD: 5/ 54 – 63
8Cas: 5B/3

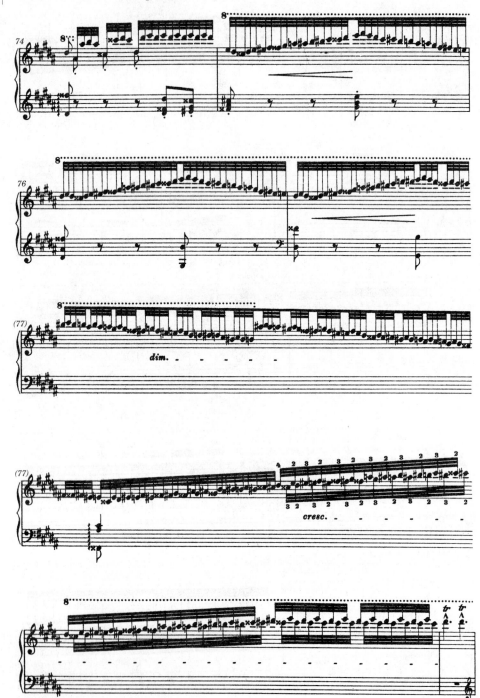

11. Richard Wagner

Die Walküre, Act III, Finale
(1856; first performed 1870)

8CD: 5/ 64 – 68
4CD: 3/ 55 – 57
8Cas: 5B/4
4Cas: 3B/4

Editor's note: Shorter Norton recording begins on page 187. This piano/vocal score includes pedal markings.

(Sie sinkt mit geschlossenen Augen, sanft ermattend, in seine Arme zurück. Er geleitet sie zart auf einen niedrigen Mooshügel
(*She sinks back with closed eyes, unconscious, in his arms. He gently bears her to a low mossy mound, which is overshadowed*

(Er betrachtet sie und schliesst
(*He looks upon her and closes*

zu liegen, über den sich eine breitästige Tanne ausstreckt.)
by a wide-spreading fir tree, and lays her upon it.)

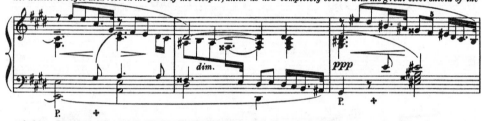

ihr den Helm: sein Auge weilt dann auf der Gestalt der Schlafenden, die er nun mit dem grossen Stahlschilde der Walküren ganz
her helmet: his eyes then rest on the form of the sleeper, which he now completely covers with the great steel shield of the

zudeckt. — Langsam kehrt er sich ab, mit einem schmerzlichen Blicke wendet er sich noch einmal um.)
Valkyrie. — He turns slowly away, then again turns round with a sorrowful look.)

12. Giuseppe Verdi	8CD: 6/ 1 – 6
Rigoletto, Act III, excerpt (1851)	4CD: 3/ 49 – 54
	8Cas: 6A/1
	4Cas: 3B/3

A lonely spot on the shore of the Mincio River, with the towers of Mantua in the background. On the left, a two-story house almost in ruins, the front of which, open to the spectator, shows a rustic inn on the ground floor: a broken staircase leads from this to a loft where stands a rough couch. On the side towards the street is a door, and a low wall extends backward from the house. Gilda and Rigoletto converse in great agitation along the road to the inn; Sparafucile is seated inside the inn. Upon reaching the inn, Rigoletto forces Gilda to watch through a fissure in the wall as the Duke enters, disguised as a cavalry officer.

strophic

Canzone (aria). "La donna è mobile"

E sempre mi-se-ro chi a lei s'af-fi-da, chi le con-fi-da
Blind in sim-plic-i-ty Men's hearts are cap-tured, Whol-ly en-rap-tured,

mal cau-to il co-re! Pur mai non sen-te-si fe-li-ce ap-pie-no
Deaf to all warn-ing. Yet full-est hap-pi-ness No man has tast-ed

chi su quel se-no non li-ba a-mo-re! La donna è mo-bil
Whose life is wast-ed Love-less and mourn-ing! Wom-an will wa-ver,

qual piuma al ven - to, mu - ta d'ac - cen - to e di pen - sier,
Turn like the weath-er, Sway like a feath-er, Nev - er the same,

e di pen - sier, e,
Nev - er the same, nev -

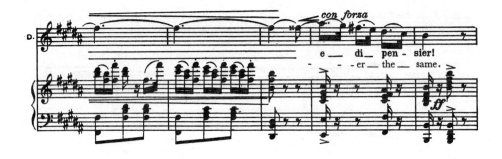

con forza

e di pen - sier!
-er the same.

(Re-enter Sparafucile with a flask of wine and two glasses, which he places on the table; then

with the hilt of his long sword he knocks on the ceiling twice. At this signal, a smiling young

girl, dressed as a Gypsy, comes bounding down the steps from
above. The Duke runs to embrace her, but she eludes him.

Meanwhile, Sparafucile goes outside the house and speaks to
Rigoletto.

Sparafucile.

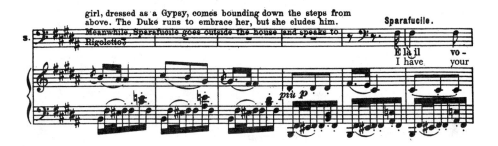

E là il vo-
I have your

Rigoletto.

str'uo - mo... Vi - ver de - e o mo - ri - re? Più
man here. Give your or - ders, I o - bey you. De-

(Sparafucile goes off behind the
house, toward the river.)

tar - di tor - ne - rò l'opra a com - pi - re.
tain him for a while, and then I'll pay you.

3 ⟨51⟩ Quartet. "Un dì, se ben rammentomi"

Gilda and Rigoletto in the street, Maddalena and the Duke on the ground floor.

Un dì, se ben ram-men - to-mi, o
One day I saw you smile at me, I

bel - la, t'in-con-tra - i... Mi piac - que di te
looked at you en-rap - tured. Your beau - ty so ex-

chie - de-re, e in-te - si che qui sta - i. Or
cit - ed me, My heart ___ was bound and cap - tured. As

sap - - pi, che d'al - lo - ra sol te ques-t'al - ma a -
no - - one else be - fore you. Sin - cere - ly I a -

son de' vez - zi tuo - - i;   con un detto, un det - to sol tu
slave me and en - chant_ me;   On - ly this one fa - vor you must

puo - i le mie pe - ne, le mie pe - ne con - so - lar.   Vieni, e
grant_ me, Come and love me, be my ra - diant guid - ing star.   I im-

sen - ti del mio co - re il fre - quente pal - pi - tar,_ con un
plore you, don't re - fuse me, Be my ra - diant, guid - ing star,_ grant me

detto, un det - to sol tu   puo - i le mie pe - ne, le mie pe - ne con - so -
this one fa - vor, I im - plore_ you, Come and love me, be my ra - diant guid - ing

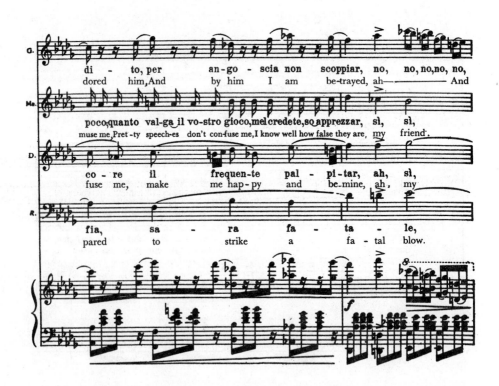

13. Clara Schumann

Scherzo, Op. 10
(c. 1838)

8CD: 5/ 69 – 76
4CD: 3/ 22 – 29
8Cas: 5B/5
4Cas: 3A/5

14. Bedřich Smetana

Vltava (The Moldau), from
Má vlast (My Fatherland)
(1874–79)

Smetana orches

Symphonic poem nonophonic

8CD: 6/ 7 – 14
4CD: 3/ 36 – 43
8Cas: 6A/2
4Cas: 3A/6

7 36

Editor's note: Smaller notes indicate an alternate version for reduced orchestra.

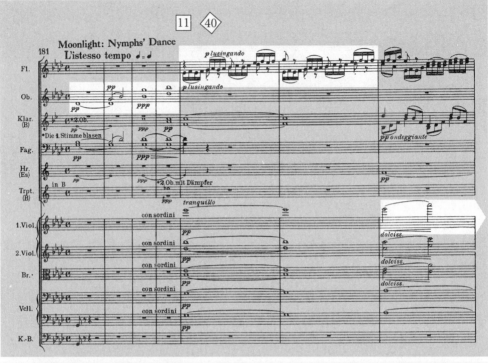

328
Kl. Fl.
1. Fl.
2. Fl.
Ob.
Klar. (A)
Fag.
Hr. (E)
Trpt. (E)
Pos. Tuba
Pk.
1. Viol.
2. Viol.
Br.
1. Vcll.
2. Vcll. K.-B.
ff
pp
sub. cresc.
sub. cresc. molto
cresc. molto

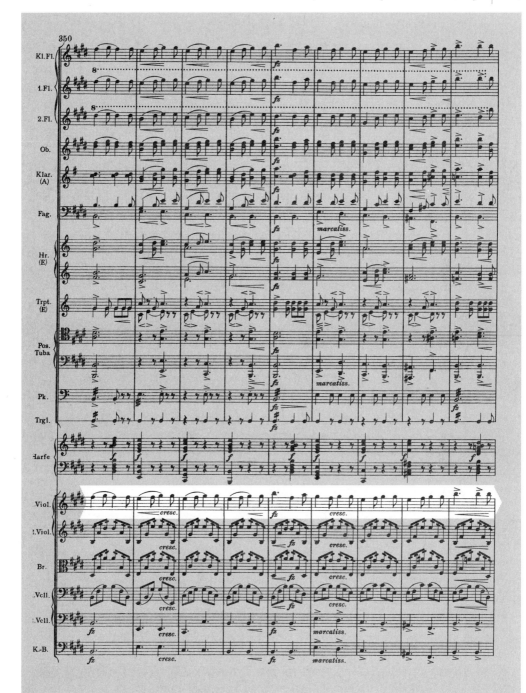

15. Johannes Brahms

Ein deutsches Requiem (A German Requiem),
Fourth Movement (1868)

8CD: 6/ 15 – 19	
4CD: 3/ 44 – 48	
8Cas: 6A/3	
4Cas: 3B/2	

homophonic,
poly, cannon.   ABACA

TEXT AND TRANSLATION

Wie lieblich sind deine
Wohnungen, Herr Zebaoth!
Meine Seele verlanget und sehnet
sich nach den Vorhöfen des Herrn;
mein Leib und Seele freuen sich
in dem lebendigen Gott.

Wie lieblich . . .

Wohl denen, die in deinem
Hause wohnen, die loben
dich immerdar!

Wie lieblich . . .

How lovely is Thy dwelling
place, O Lord of Hosts!
My soul longs and even
faints for the courts of the Lord;
my flesh and soul rejoice
in the living God.

How lovely . . .

Blessed are they that live in
Thy house, that praise
Thee evermore!

How lovely . . .

16. Johannes Brahms

Symphony No. 3 in F major,
Fourth Movement (1883)

8CD: 6/ 20 – 31
8Cas: 6A/4

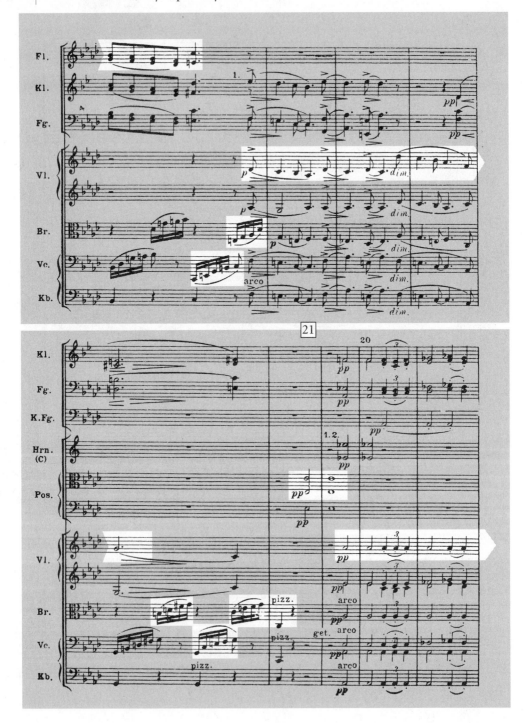

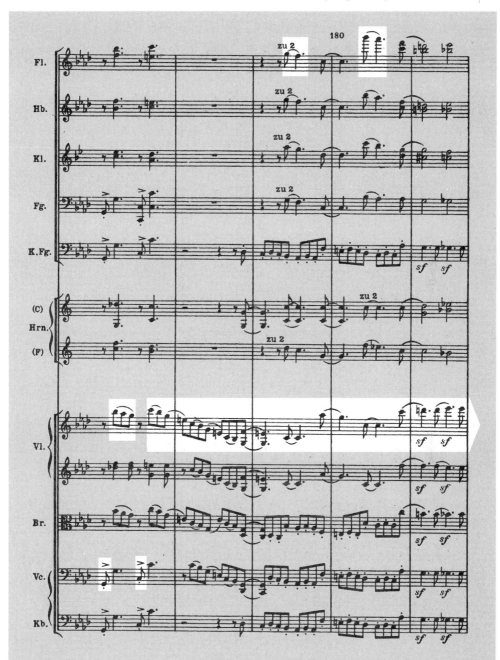

427-9

31

Un poco sostenuto

17. Georges Bizet

Carmen, Act I, excerpt (1875)

8CD: 6/ 32 – 39
8Cas: 6B/1

Scene No. 3

(The relief appears:

first a bugler and fifer, then a crowd of street-boys. — Following the latter, Lieutenant Zuniga and

Corporal Don José, then the dragoons. — During Street-boys' Chorus, the relief forms in front of the

guard going off duty.)

Recitative

Ju - pe bleue et nat - te tom - ban - te.
"Light blue skirt and ver-y long braids!"

Don José.

Tu ne ré - ponds rien à ce - la? Je ré - ponds que c'est
Well, am I right a - bout that? I ad - mit you are

vrai, je ré - ponds que je l'ai - me!
right. I con - fess, she's the girl I love.

Recit.

Quant aux ou - vri - e - res d'i - ci, Quant à leur beau-
And as for the fac - to - ry girls, When you hear the

té, les voi - ci! Et vous pou - vez ju - ger vous - mê - me.
bell, they'll be here. Then you can judge their looks quite well.

attacca subito.

Scene No. 4

Scene No. 5

18. Peter Ilyich Tchaikovsky

The Nutcracker, Three Dances from Act II
(1892)

8CD: 6/ 40 – 48
4CD: 4/ 1 – 3
8Cas: 6A/5–7
4Cas: 4A/1

March

Dance of the Sugar Plum Fairy

Trepak (Russian Dance)

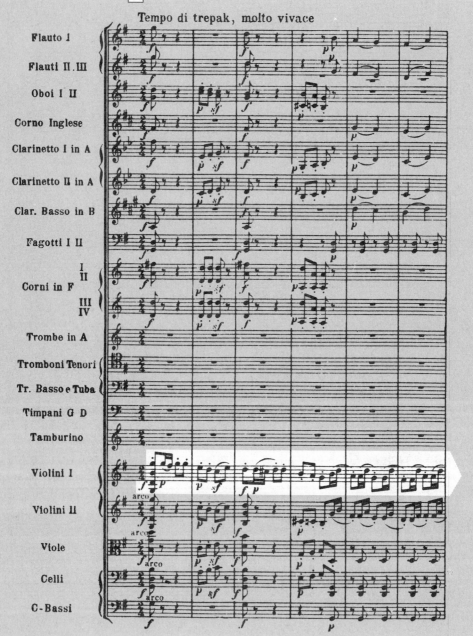

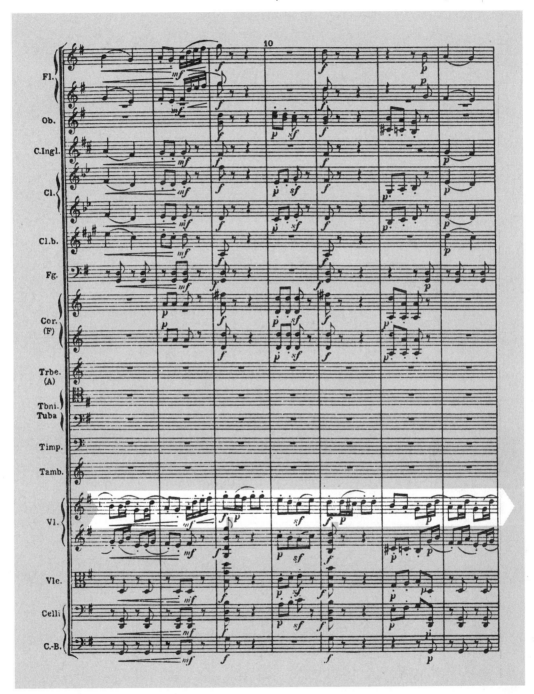

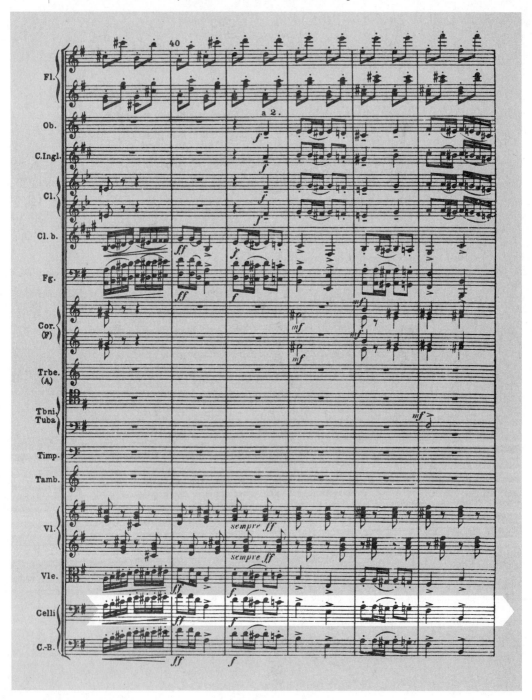

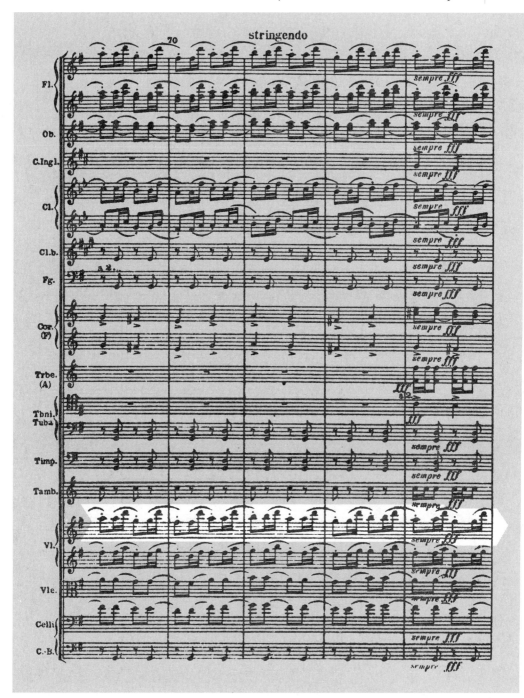

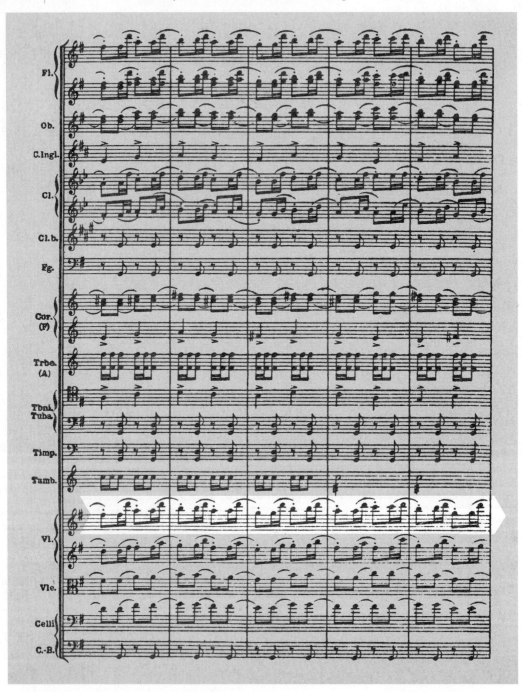

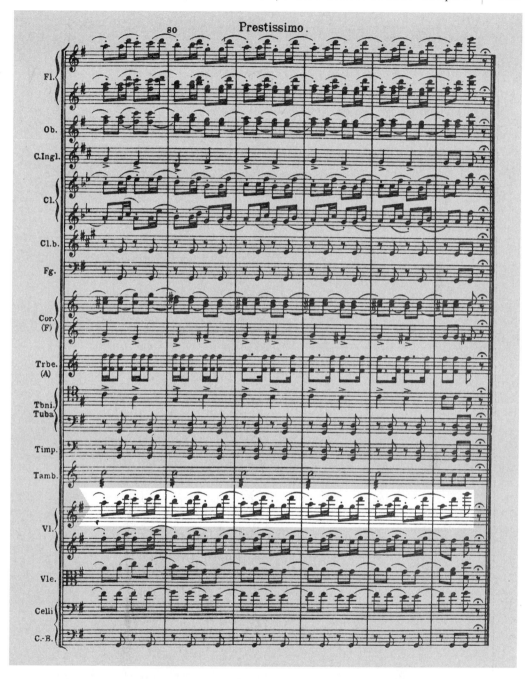

19. Antonín Dvořák

Symphony No. 9 in E minor
(From the New World),
Second Movement (1893)

8CD: 6/ 49 – 51
8Cas: 6B/2

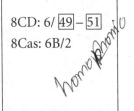

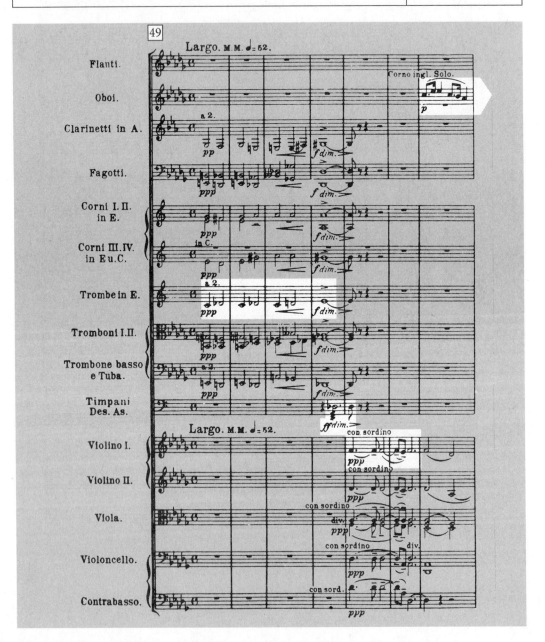

20. Ruggero Leoncavallo

Pagliacci, Act I, Canio's Aria
(1892)

8CD: 6/ 52 – 53
8Cas: 6B/3
MasterWorks

Canio

Re - ci - tar! Men - tre pre - so dal de - li -
To per - form! When my head's whir - ling with an -

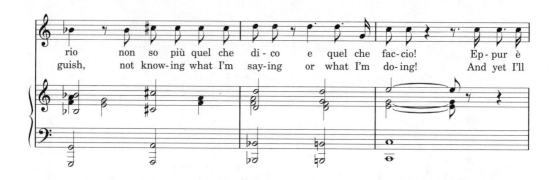

rio non so più quel che di - co e quel che fac - cio! Ep - pur è
guish, not know-ing what I'm say-ing or what I'm do-ing! And yet I'll

string. un poco   (angrily)

d'uo - po... sfor - za - ti! Bah! sei tu for-se un uom?
have to force my - self! Bah, can't you be a man?

col canto   *precipitato*

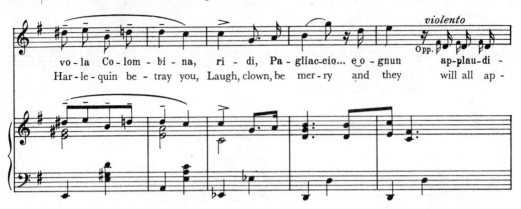

vo - la Co - lom - bi - na, ri - di, Pa - gliac-cio... e o-gnun ap-plau-di -

Har - le - quin be - tray you, Laugh, clown, be mer-ry and they will all ap -

rà! Tra - mu - ta in laz - zi lo spa - smo e il pian - to;

plaud! You must trans - form your des - pair in - to laugh - ter;

in u - na smor-fia il sin - ghiozzo e'l do - lor... Ah!

And make a jest of your sob-bing, of your pain... Ah!

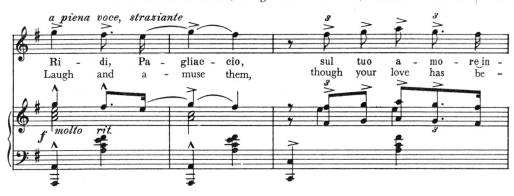

Ri - di, Pa - gliac - cio,   sul tuo a - mo - re in -
Laugh and a - muse them,   though your love has be -

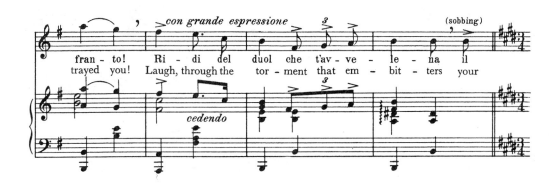

fran - to! Ri - di del duol che t'av - ve - le - na il
trayed you! Laugh, through the tor - ment that em - bit - ters your

cor! _____
heart! _____

stage, he pushes it roughly, as if not wishing to enter; then, seized by a new

cresc. sempre

fit of sobbing, he again buries his face in his

f

poco rit. con dolore

p

(The curtain begins to fall slowly)

hands; takes three or four steps towards the curtain, from which he had

rianimando

recoiled in fury, and [on these chords] enters and disappears)

rit. ed accentato molto

marcato il canto

r.h.

End of Act I

21. Gustav Mahler

Das Lied von der Erde (The Song of the Earth),
Third Movement (1908–9)

3. *Von der Jugend (Of Youth)*

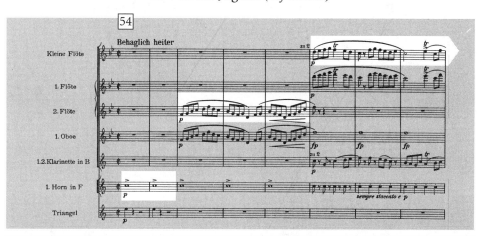

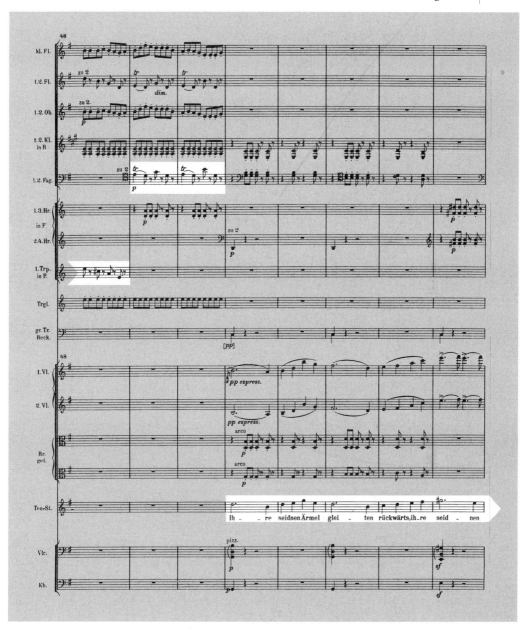

TEXT AND TRANSLATION

Mitten in dem kleinen Teiche steht ein Pavillon aus grünem und aus weissem Porzellan.	In the middle of the little pool stands a pavilion of green and of white porcelain.
Wie der Rücken eines Tigers wölbt die Brücke sich aus Jade zu dem Pavillon hinüber.	Like the back of a tiger the bridge of jade arches over to the pavilion.
In dem Häuschen sitzen Freunde, schön gekleidet, trinken, plaudern, manche schreiben Verse nieder.	In the little house, friends are sitting beautifully dressed, drinking, chatting; several are writing verses.
Ihre seidnen Ärmel gleiten rückwärts, ihre seidnen Mützen hocken lustig tief im Nacken.	Their silken sleeves slip backwards, their silken caps perch gaily on the back of their necks.
Auf des kleinen Teiches stiller Wasserfläche zeigt sich alles wunderlich im Spiegelbilde.	On the little pool's still surface everything appears fantastically in a mirror image.
Alles auf dem Kopfe stehend in dem Pavillon aus grünem und aus weissem Porzellan;	Everything is standing on its head in the pavilion of green and of white porcelain;

wie ein Halbmond scheint die Brücke
umgekehrt der Bogen.
Freunde, schön gekleidet,
   trinken, plaudern.
	like a half-moon stands the bridge,
	upside-down its arch.
	Friends, beautifully dressed, are
	   drinking, chatting.

22. Claude Debussy

Prélude à "L'après-midi d'un faune"
(Prelude to "The Afternoon of a Faun") (1894)

8CD: 7/ 1 – 5
4CD: 3/ 58 – 62
8Cas: 7A/1
4Cas: 3B/5

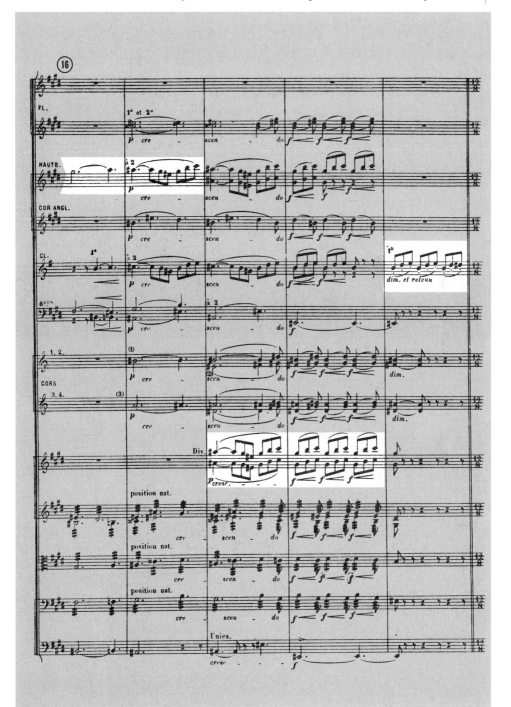

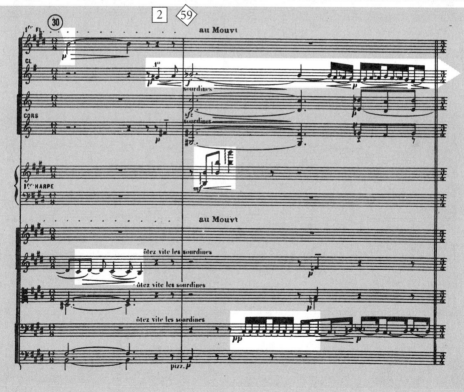

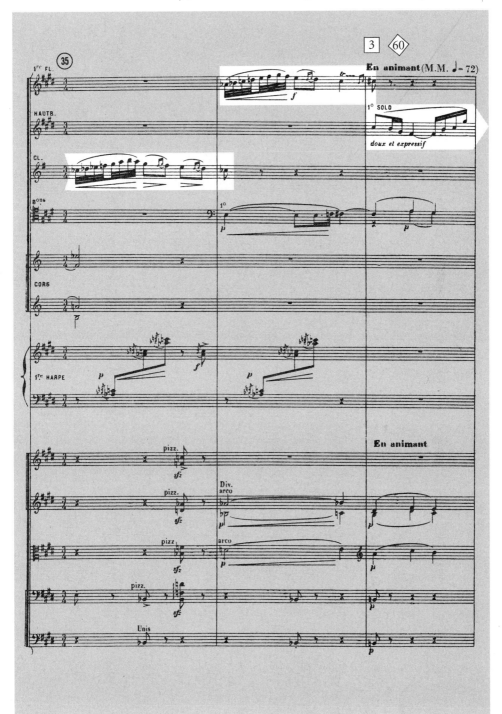

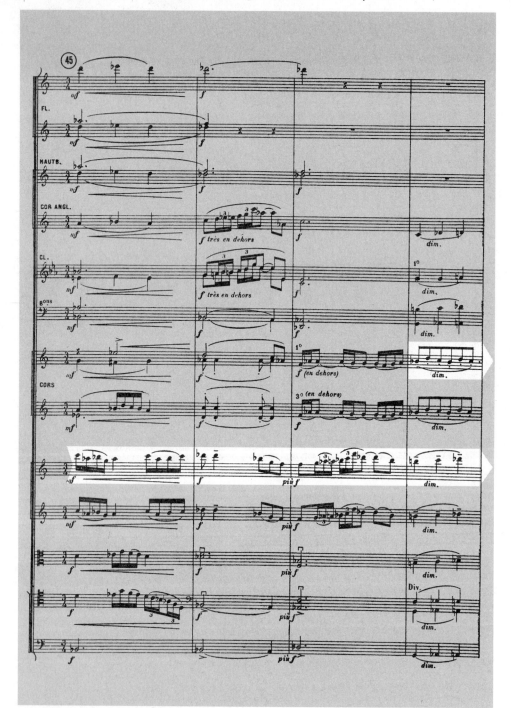

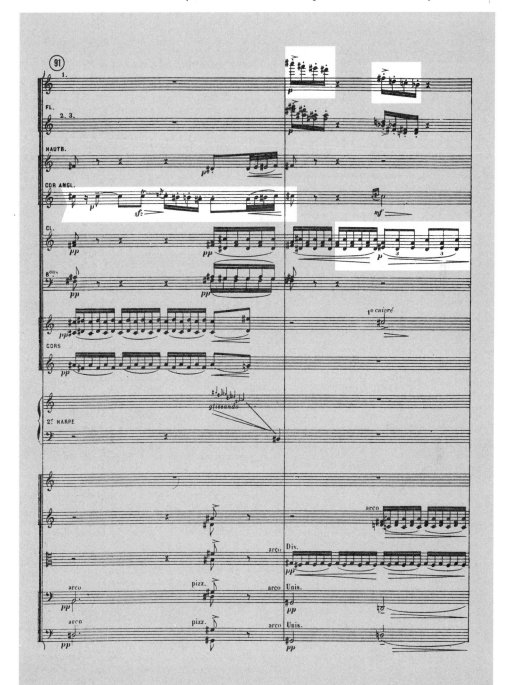

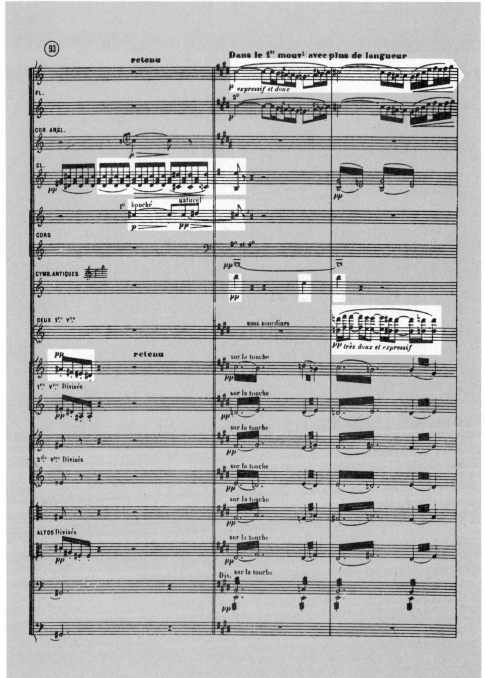

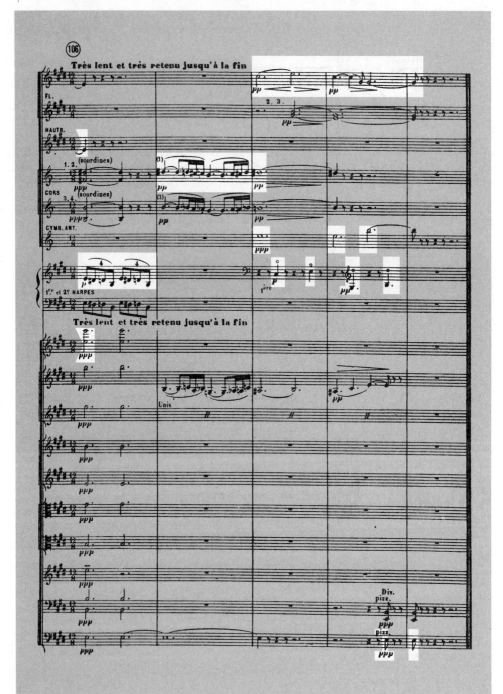

23. Richard Strauss

Der Rosenkavalier (The Cavalier of the Rose),
Act III, Trio (1909-10)

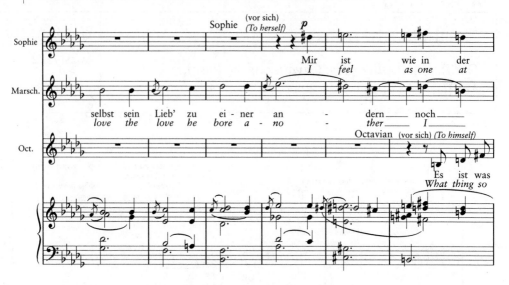

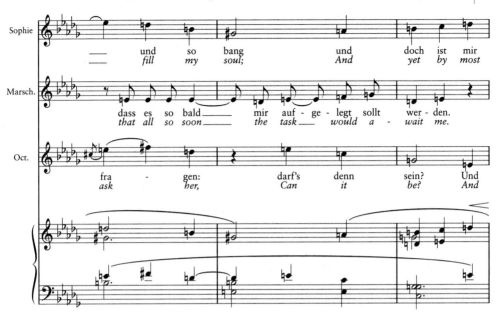

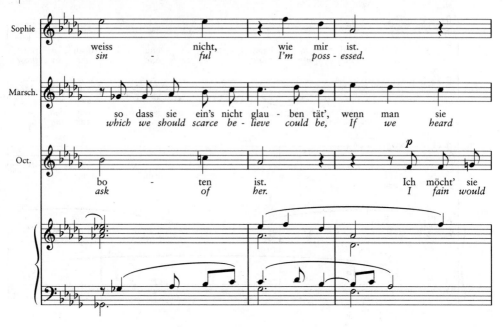

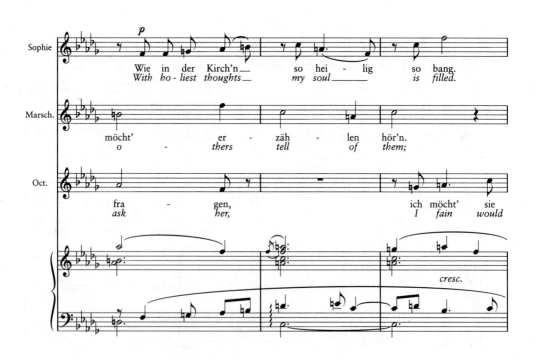

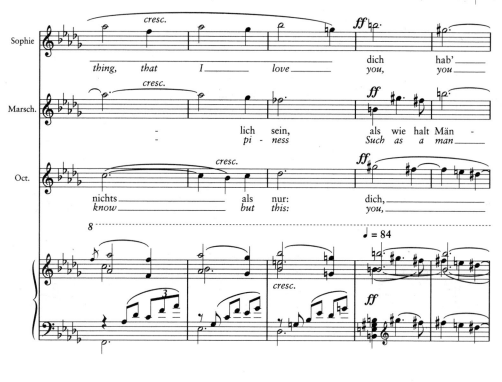

(Die Marschallin geht leise links hinein,
die Beiden bemerken es gar nicht.)
*(The Princess goes quietly into the room on the left;
the two others do not notice her.)*

24. Amy Cheney Beach

Violin Sonata in A minor, Second Movement (1896)

8CD: 7/ 8 – 10
8Cas: 7A/3

Tempo I.

25. Scott Joplin

Maple Leaf Rag
(1899)

8CD: 7/ 11 – 15
4CD: 4/ 27 – 31
8Cas: 7A/4
4Cas: 4A/6

Editor's note: The Norton recording, from a Joplin piano roll, features embellishments added by the composer.

26. Arnold Schoenberg

Pierrot lunaire, Op. 21,
Nos. 18 and 21 (1912)

8CD: 7/ 16 – 19
4CD: 4/ ◇13◇ – ◇14◇
8Cas: 7A/5–6
4Cas: 4A/3
MasterWorks

No. 18. *Der Mondfleck*

TEXT AND TRANSLATION

Einen weissen Fleck des hellen
  Mondes
Auf dem Rücken seines schwarzen Rockes,
So spaziert Pierrot im lauen Abend,
Aufzusuchen Glück und Abenteuer.

Plötzlich stört ihn was an seinem Anzug,
Er besieht sich rings und findet richtig—
Einen weissen Fleck des hellen Mondes
Auf dem Rücken seines schwarzen Rockes.

Warte! denkt er: das ist so ein Gipsfleck!
Wischt und wischt, doch—bringt ihn nicht
  herunter!
Und so geht er, giftgeschwollen, weiter,
Reibt und reibt bis an den frühen Morgen—
Einen weissen Fleck des hellen Mondes.

With a fleck of white—from the bright
  moon—
on the back of his black jacket,
Pierrot strolls about in the mild evening
seeking his fortune and adventure.

Suddenly something strikes him as wrong,
he checks his clothes and sure enough finds
a fleck of white—from the bright moon—
on the back of his black jacket.

Damn! he thinks: that's a spot of plaster!
Wipes and wipes, but—he can't get it
  off.
And so goes on his way, his pleasure poisoned,
rubs and rubs till the early morning—
a fleck of white—from the bright moon.

No. 21. *O alter Duft*

TEXT AND TRANSLATION

O alter Duft aus Märchenzeit,
Berauschest wieder meine Sinne!
Ein närrisch Heer von Schelmerein
Durchschwirrt die leichte Luft.

Ein glückhaft Wünschen macht mich froh
Nach Freuden, die ich lang verachtet:
O alter Duft aus Märchenzeit,
Berauschest wieder mich!

All meinen Unmut geb ich preis:
Aus meinem sonnumrahmten Fenster
Beschau ich frei die liebe Welt
Und träum hinaus in selge Weiten . . .
O alter Duft aus Märchenzeit!

O scent of fabled yesteryear,
intoxicating my senses once again!
A foolish swarm of idle fancies
pervades the gentle air.

A happy desire makes me yearn for
joys that I have long scorned:
O scent of fabled yesteryear,
intoxicating me again.

All my ill humor is dispelled:
from my sun-drenched window
I look out freely on the lovely world
and dream of beyond the horizon . . .
O scent of fabled yesteryear!

27. Charles Ives

The Things Our Fathers Loved (1917)

8CD: 7/ [20] – [21]
8Cas: 7A/7

I think there must be a place in the soul all made of tunes, of

tunes of long a - go; I hear the or - gan on the Main Street cor - ner, Aunt

Sa - rah humming Gos - pels; Sum - mer eve - nings, The

28. Maurice Ravel

Rapsodie espagnole (Spanish Rhapsody),
Fourth Movement, *Feria* (1907–8)

8CD: 7/ 22 – 27
8Cas: 7A/8

(*) **Glissez** en effleurant la corde *du côté du chevalet*

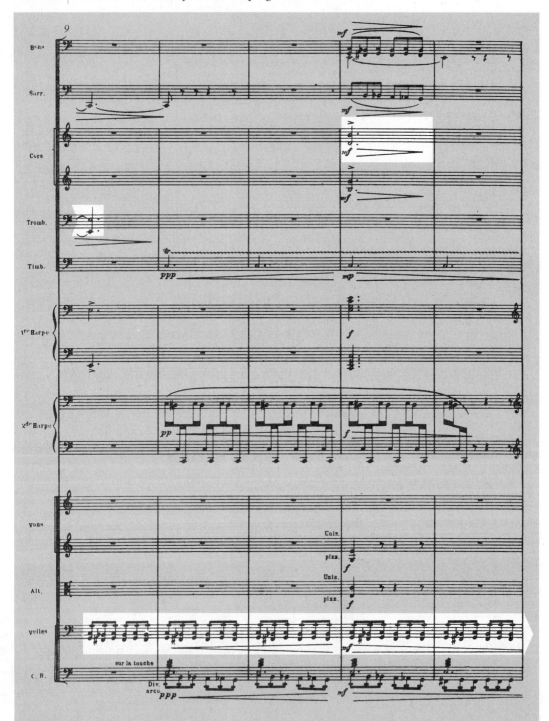

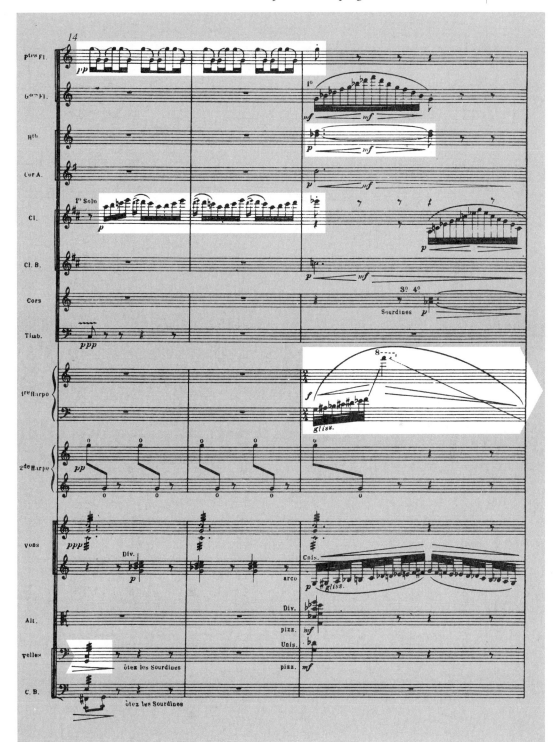

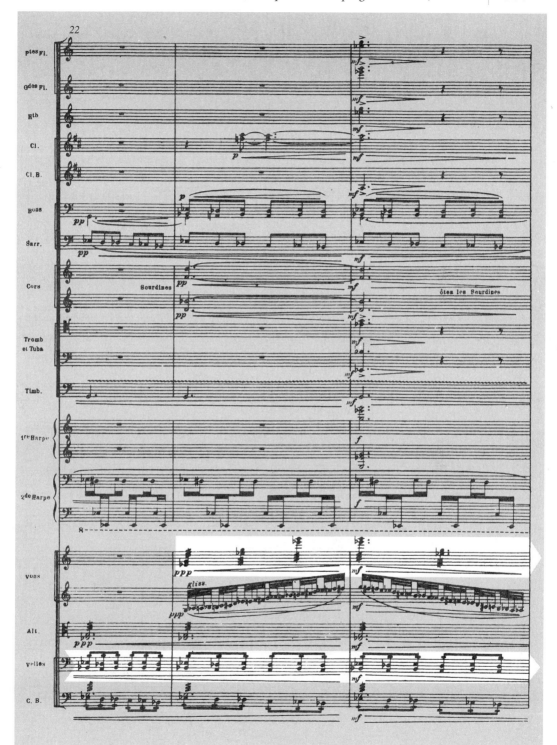

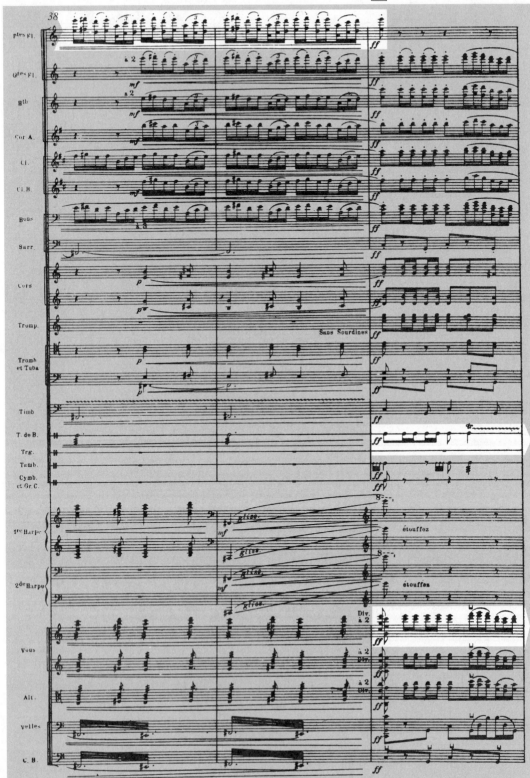

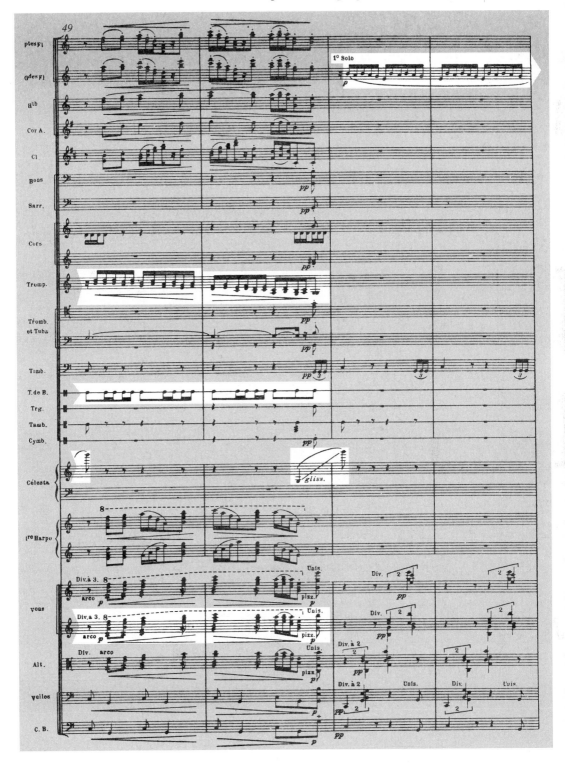

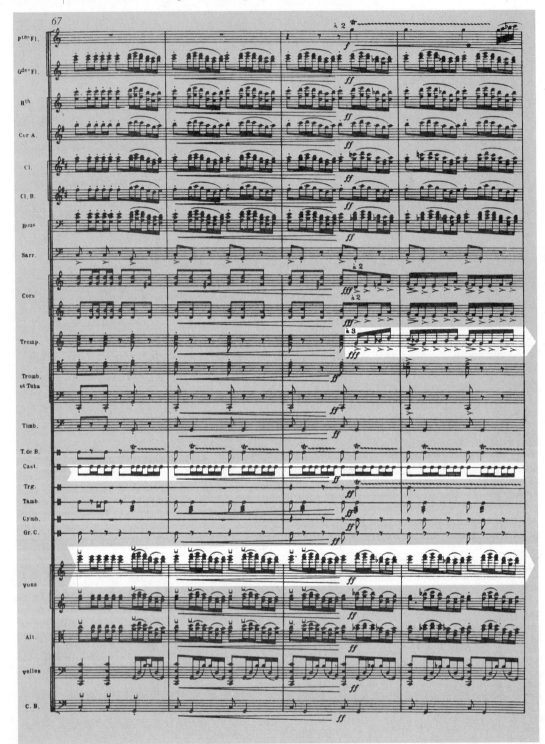

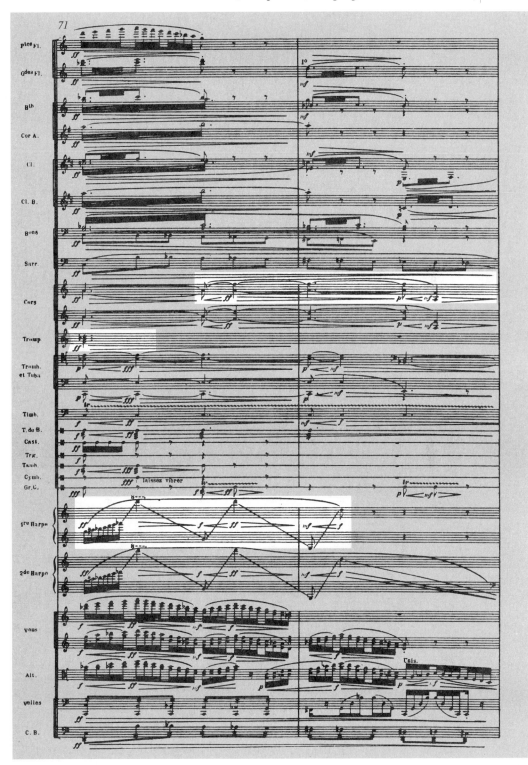

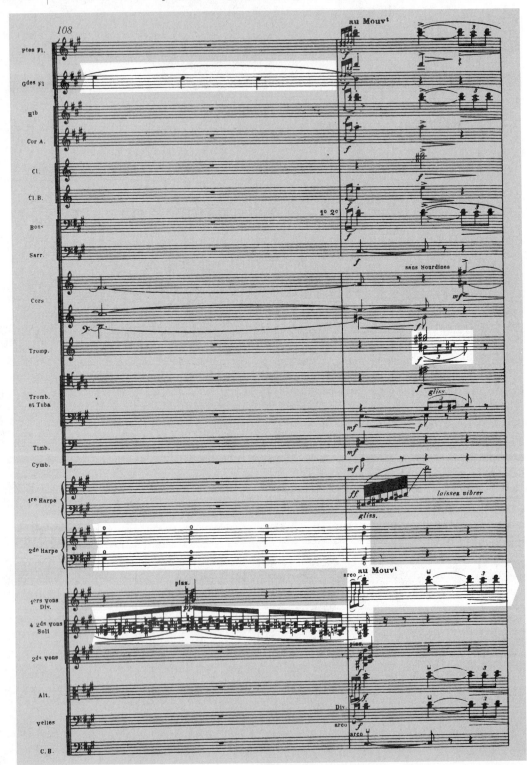

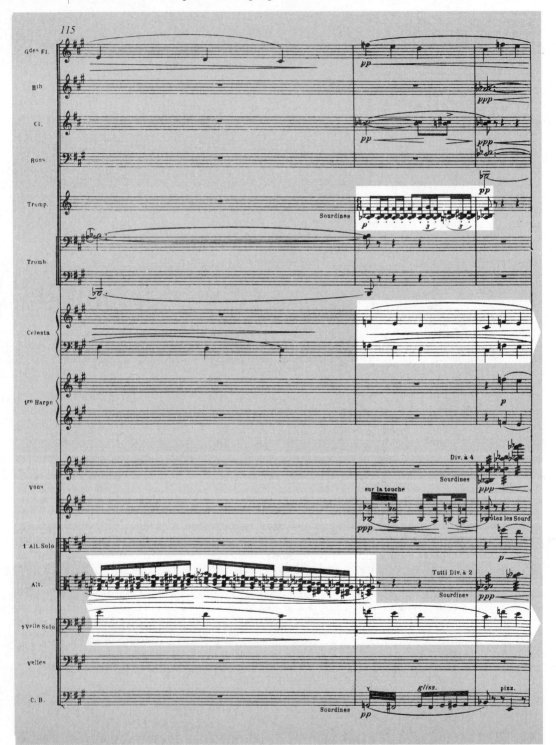

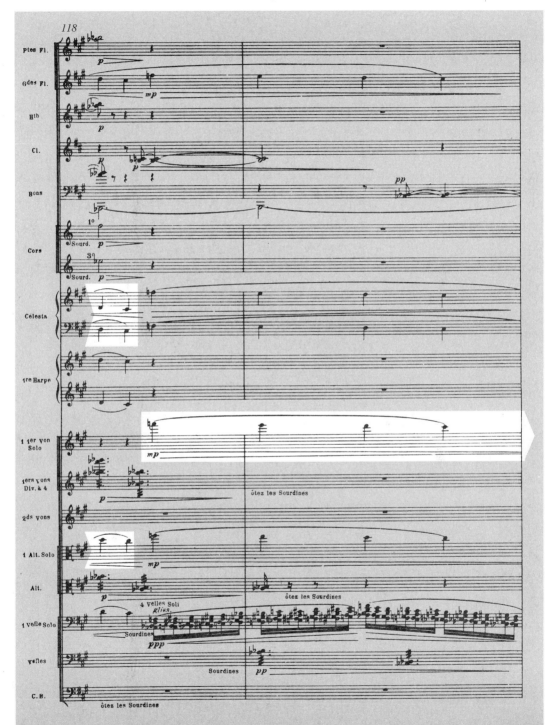

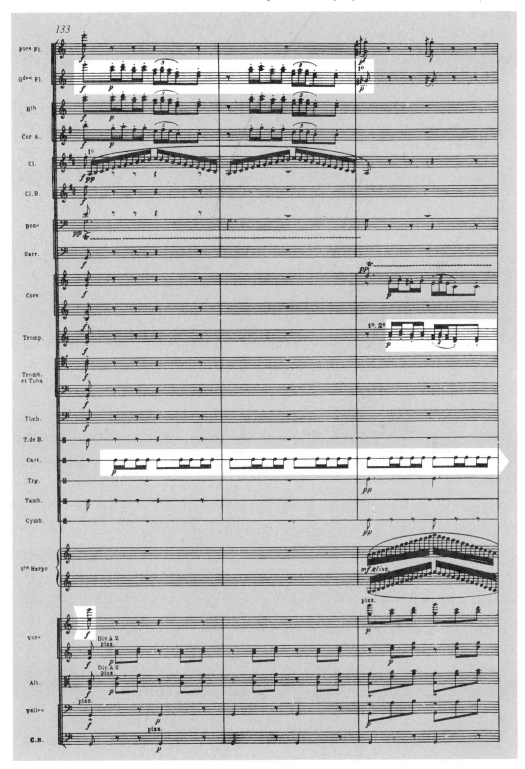

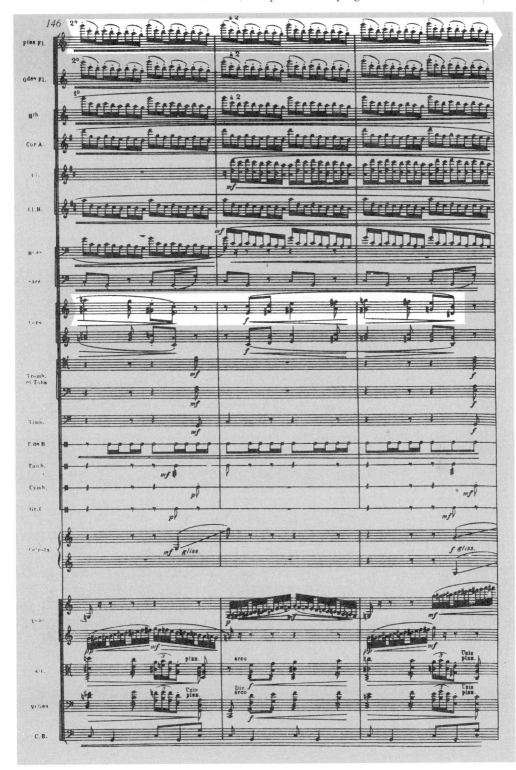

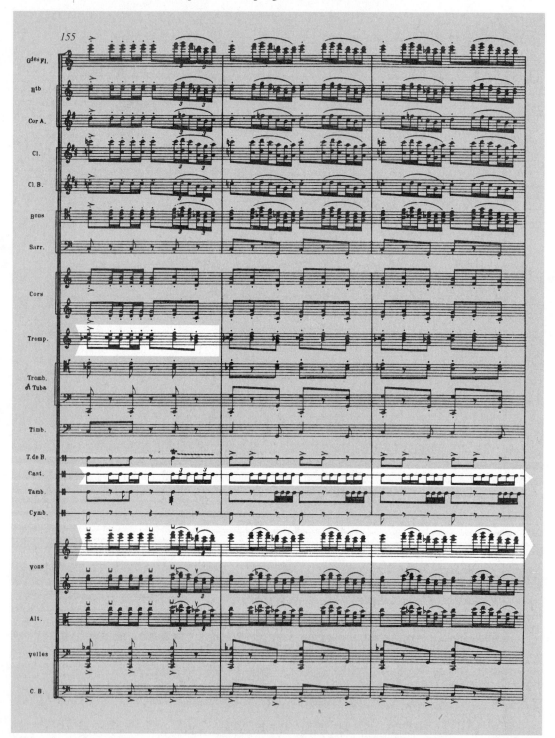

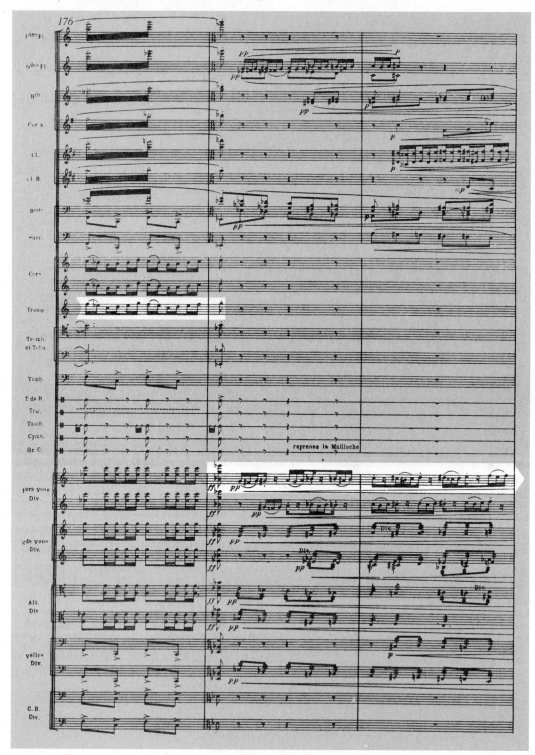

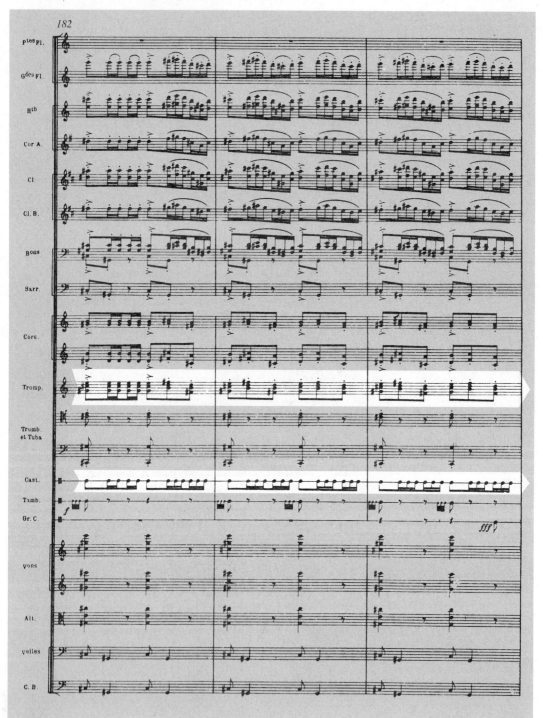

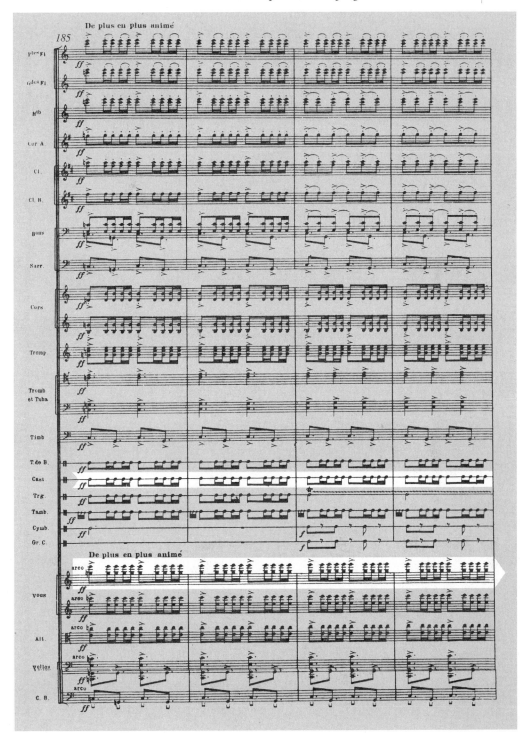

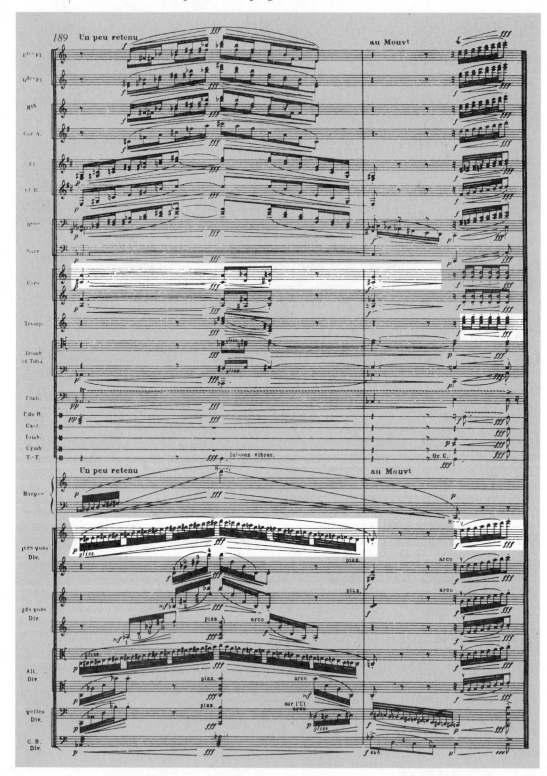

29. Béla Bartók

Concerto for Orchestra, Fourth Movement,
Interrupted Intermezzo (1943)

8CD: 7/ 28 – 34
4CD: 4/ 15 – 21
8Cas: 7A/9
4Cas: 4A/4

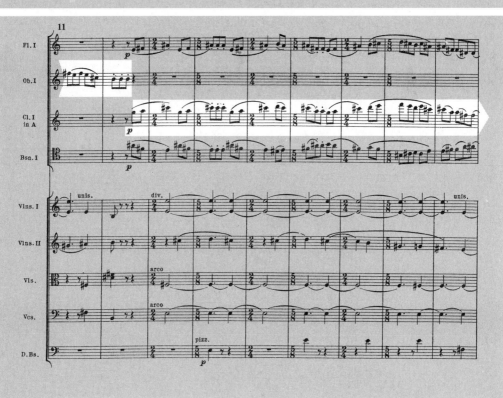

* If the Flute has no low *b*, 1st Bassoon will play: and Flute tacet.

*real sound:

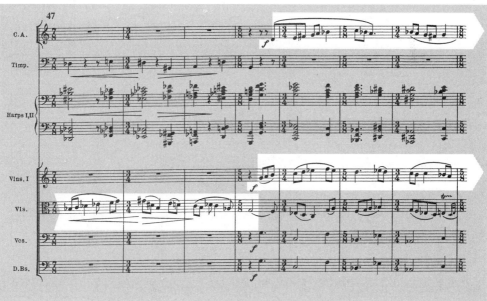

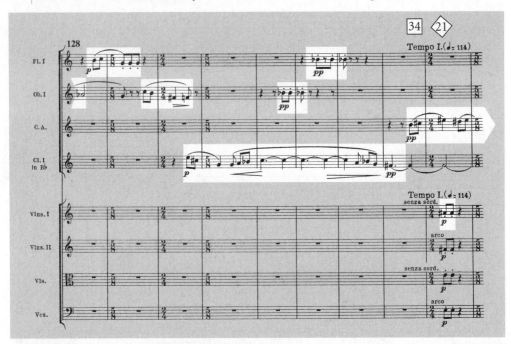

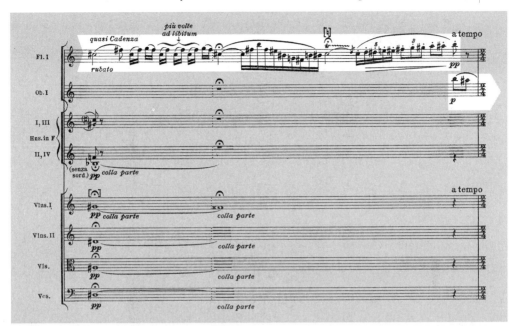

30. Igor Stravinsky

Petrushka, First Tableau (1911)

8CD: 7/ 35 – 50
4CD: 4/ ◇4 – ◇12
8Cas: 7B/1
4Cas: 4A/2
MasterWorks

"The Shrovetide Fair"

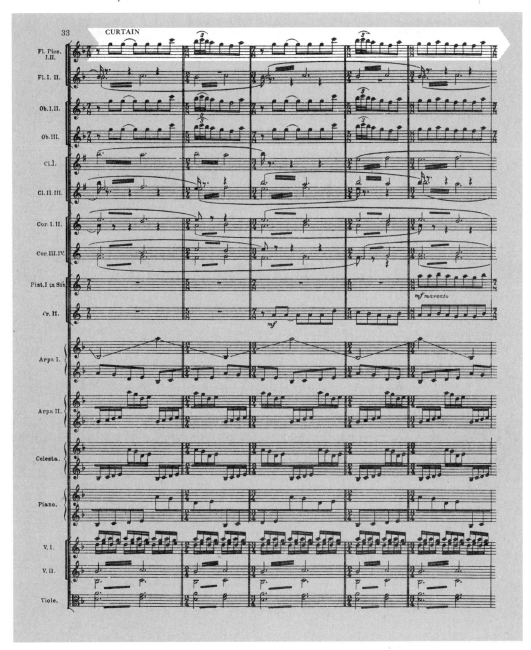

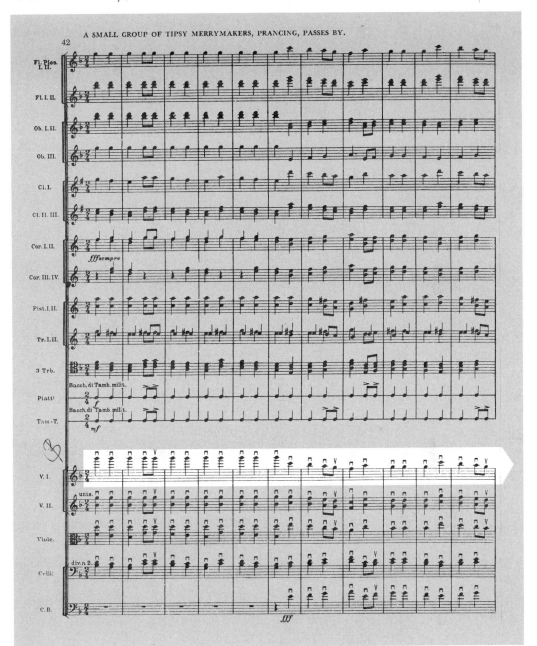

A SMALL GROUP OF TIPSY MERRYMAKERS, PRANCING, PASSES BY.

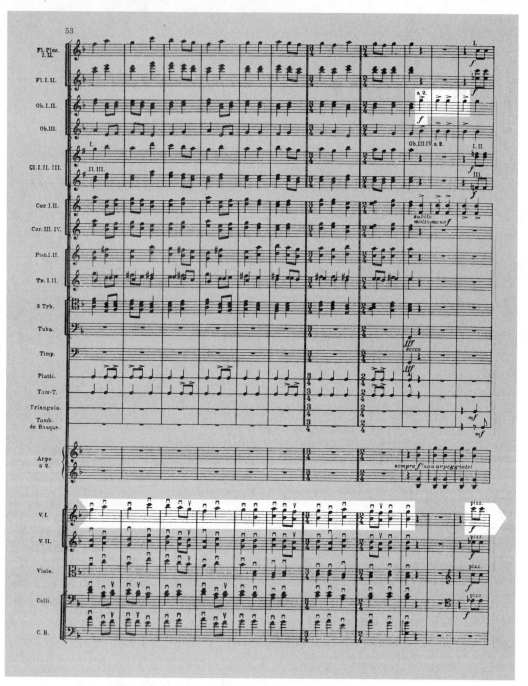

76 ENTERTAINS THE CROWD FROM THE HEIGHT OF HIS BOOTH.

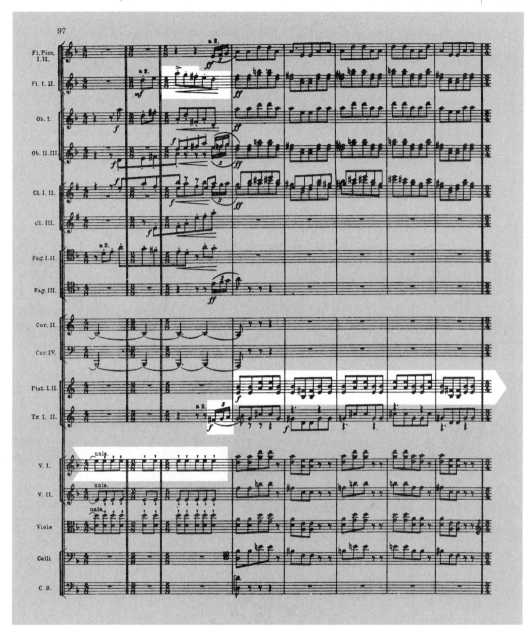

39 **8**

THE STREET DANCER DANCES,
BEATING TIME ON THE TRIANGLE.

*THE ORGAN-GRINDER, CONTINUING TO TURN THE CRANK WITH ONE HAND, PLAYS
THE CORNET WITH THE OTHER.

*THE ORGAN-GRINDER RESUMES PLAYING THE CORNET.

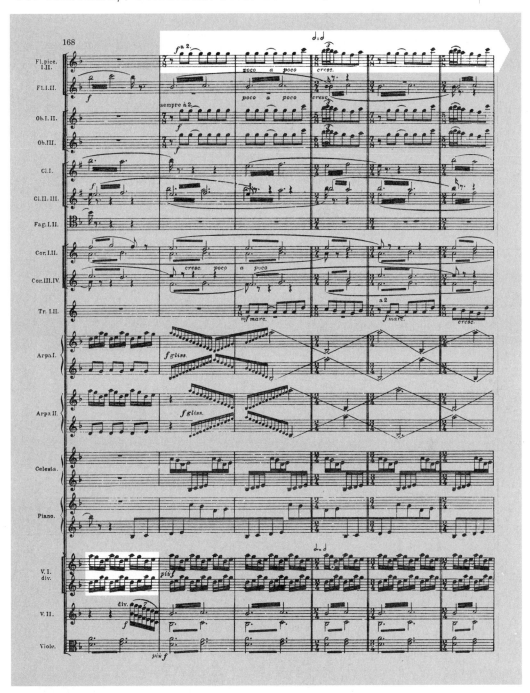

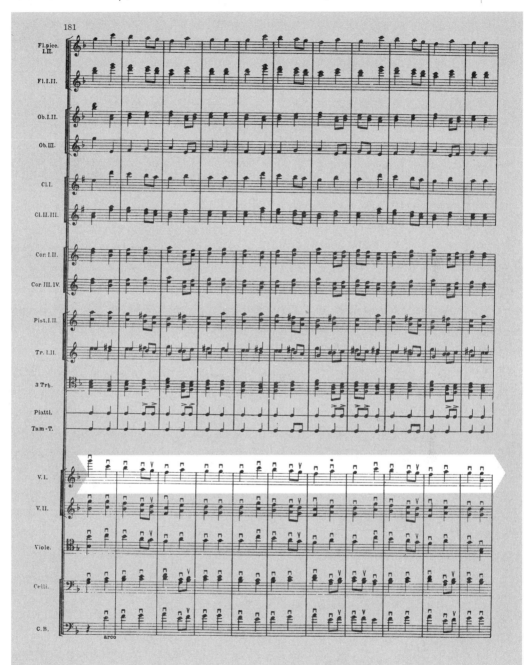

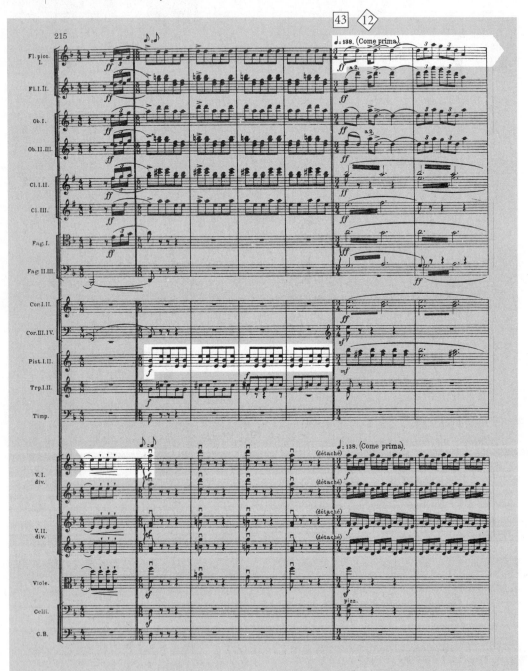

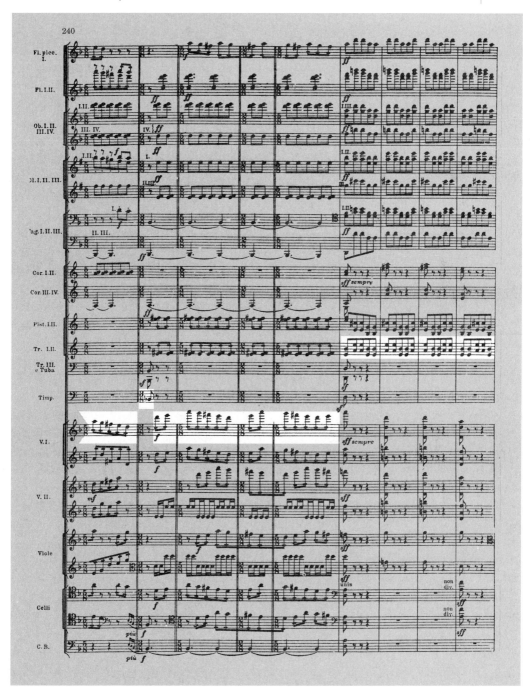

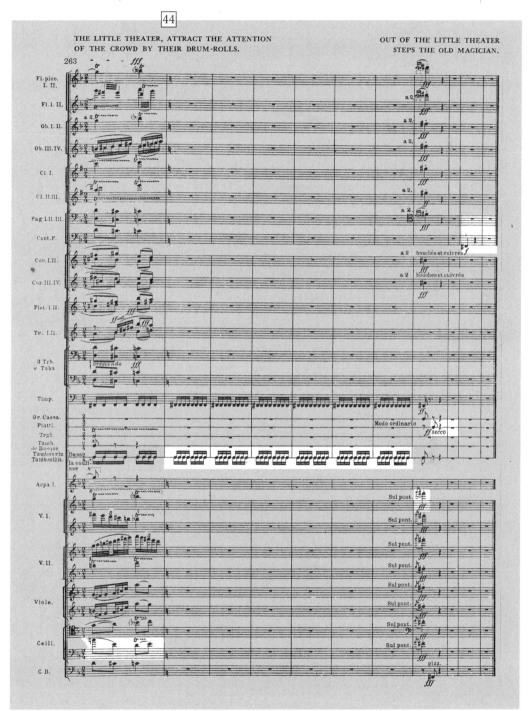

"The Magic Trick"

THE MAGICIAN PLAYS THE FLUTE.

THE CURTAIN OF THE LITTLE THEATER OPENS, AND THE CROWD SEES THREE PUPPETS:
PETRUSHKA, A MOOR, AND A BALLERINA.

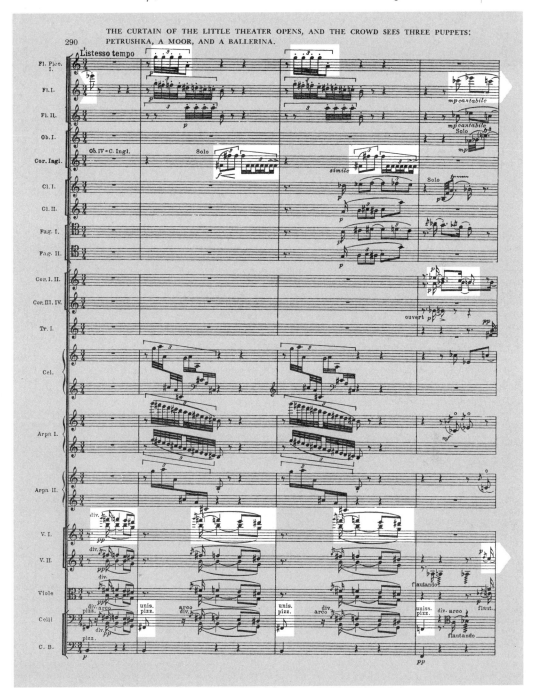

THE MAGICIAN ANIMATES THEM BY
TOUCHING THEM WITH HIS FLUTE.

"Russian Dance"

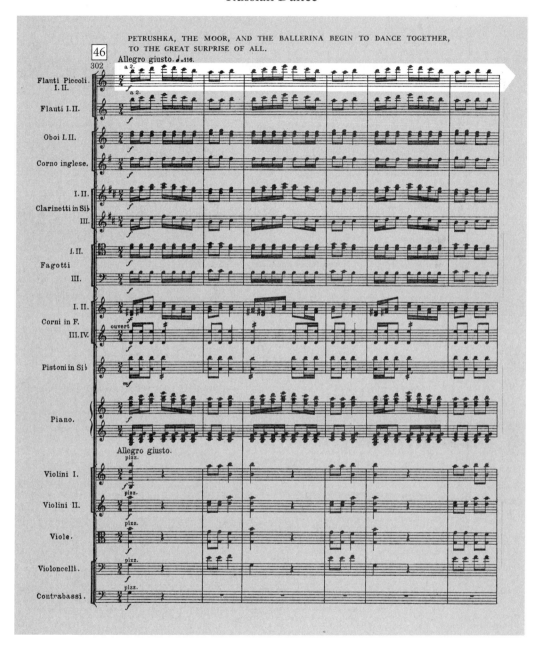

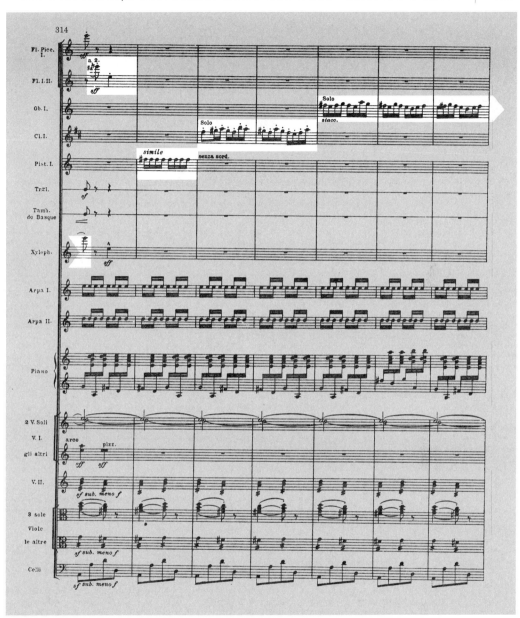

48

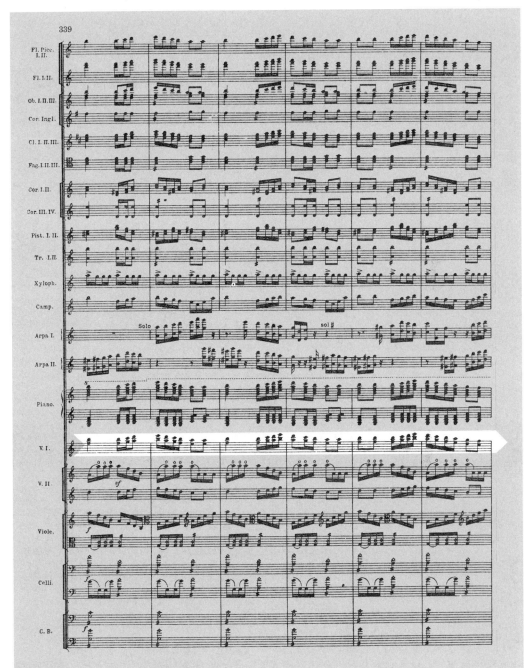

Editor's note: The last measure on this page is not played when continuing to the Second Tableau.

*) Son lointain, mais violent. Réglez selon l'acoustique de la sale.

Editor's note: The Norton recording stops in the second measure of this page at the fermata.

31. Anton Webern

Symphony, Op. 21, Second Movement (1928)

8CD: 7/ 51 – 53

8Cas: 7B/2

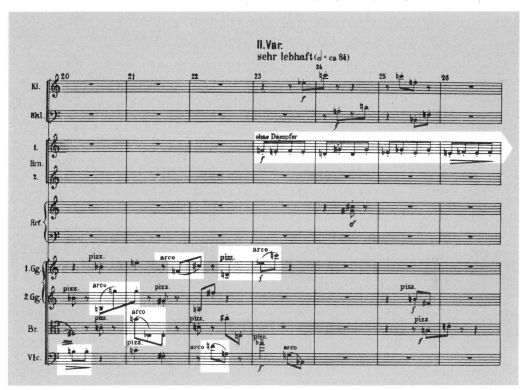

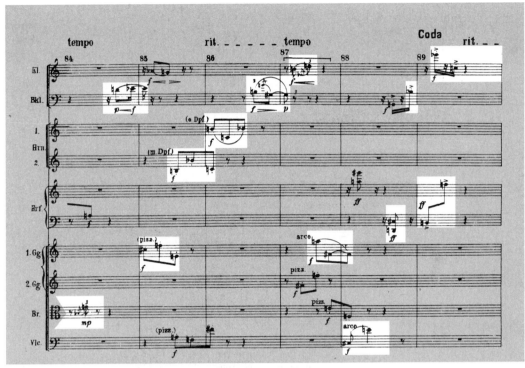

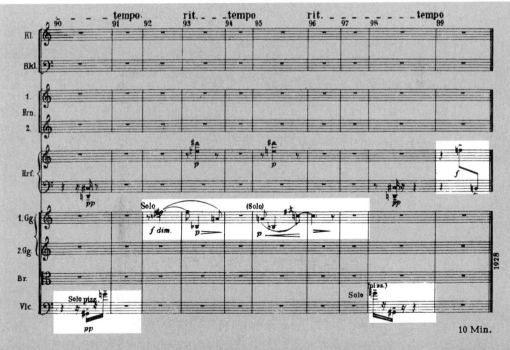

forms: Baroque suite.
- Rhapsody on 3 chords
- Military march.
- passacaglia

32. Alban Berg

Wozzeck, Act III, Scenes 4 and 5 (1922)

8CD: 7/ 54 – 57
8Cas: 7B/3

Wieder langsamer, aber nicht schleppend

255

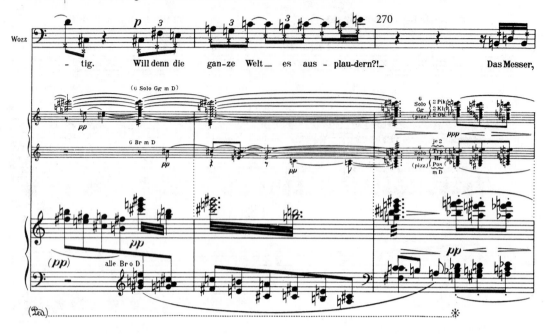

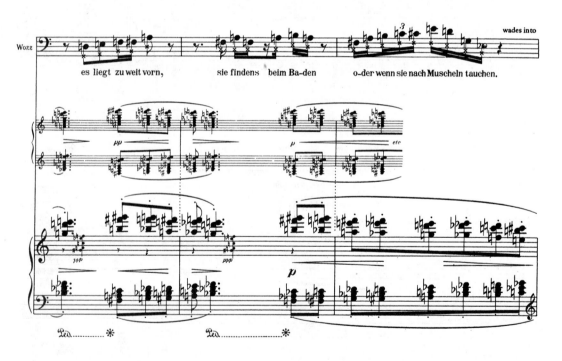

The **Captain** follows the Doctor (speaks)

The **Doctor** (stands still): *p* Hören Sie? Dort!

Hauptmann: *p* Jesus! Das war ein Ton. (also stands still)

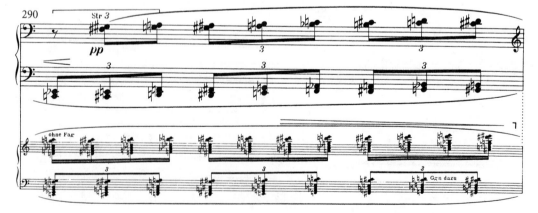

Doktor (pointing to the lake): Ja, dort!   **Hauptmann:** Es ist das Wasser

im Teich.   Das Wasser ruft.   Es ist schon lange niemand ertrunken.

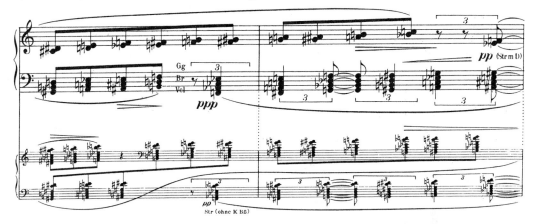

Hauptmann: Kommen Sie, Doktor!   Es   ist

295

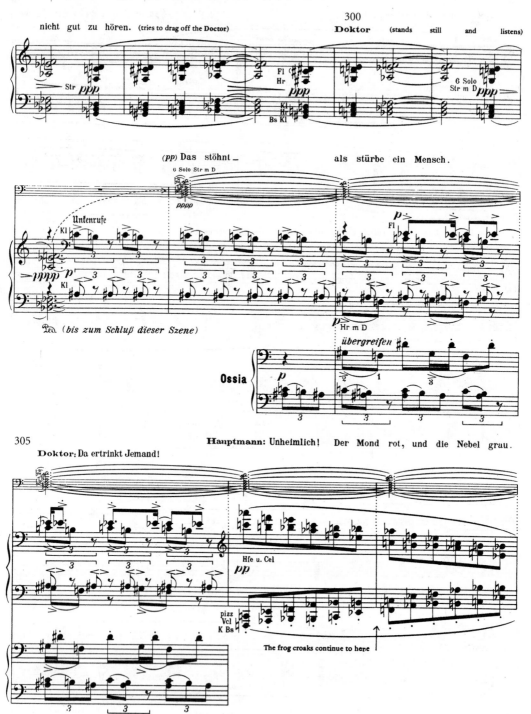

5th (last) Scene   In front of Marie's house (bright morning, sunshine)

Flowing 8ths, but with much rubato

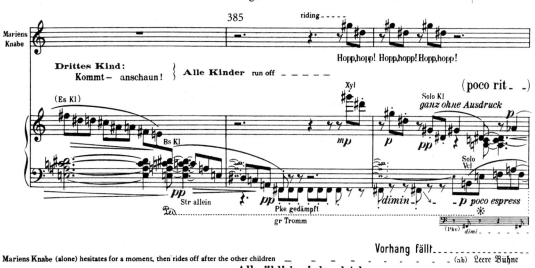

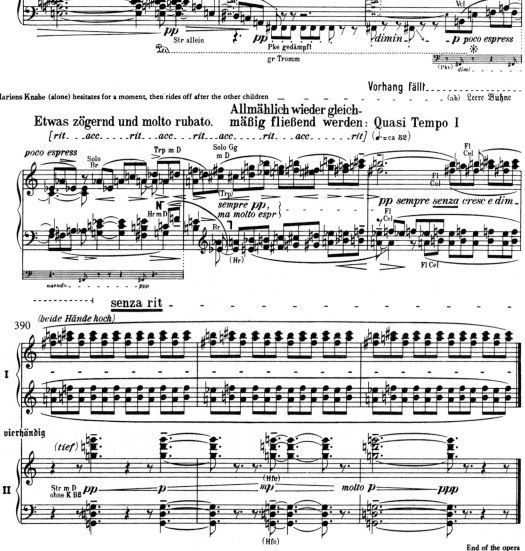

End of the opera

TEXT AND TRANSLATION

SCENE FOUR
INVENTION ON A CHORD OF SIX NOTES
PATH IN THE WOOD BY THE POND. MOONLIGHT, AS BEFORE.
(WOZZECK STUMBLES HURRIEDLY IN, THEN STOPS, LOOKING AROUND FOR SOMETHING.)

WOZZECK

Das Messer? Wo ist das Messer? Ich hab's
dagelassen. Näher, noch näher. Mir graut's
. . . da regt sich was. Still! Alles still und tot.

The knife? Where is the knife? I left it
there. Around here somewhere. I'm terrified
. . . something's moving. Silence. Everything
silent and dead.

(SHOUTING)

Mörder! Mörder!

Murderer! Murderer!

(WHISPERING AGAIN)

Ha! Da ruft's. Nein, ich selbst.

Ah! Someone called. No, it was only me.

(STILL LOOKING, HE STAGGERS A FEW STEPS FURTHER AND STUMBLES AGAINST THE CORPSE.)

Marie! Marie! Was hast du für eine rote Schnur
um den Hals? Hast dir das rote Halsband
verdient, wie die Ohrringlein, mit deiner
Sünde! Was hängen dir die schwarzen Haare
so wild? Mörder! Mörder! Sie werden nach
mir suchen. Das Messer verrät mich!

Marie! Marie! What's that red cord around
your neck? Was the red necklace payment
for your sins, like the earrings? Why's your
dark hair so wild about you? Murderer!
Murderer! They will come and look for me.
The knife will betray me!

(LOOKS FOR IT IN A FRENZY)

Da, da ist's!

Here! Here it is!

(AT THE POND)

So! Da hinunter!

There! Sink to the bottom!

(THROWS THE KNIFE INTO THE POND)

Es taucht ins dunkle Wasser wie ein Stein.

It plunges into the dark water like a stone.

(THE MOON APPEARS, BLOOD-RED, FROM BEHIND THE CLOUDS. WOZZECK LOOKS UP.)

Aber der Mond verrät mich, der Mond ist blutig.
Will denn die ganze Welt es ausplaudern?
Das Messer, es liegt zu weit vorn, sie finden's
beim Baden oder wenn sie nach Muscheln tauchen.

But the moon will betray me: the moon is blood-
stained. Is the whole world going to
incriminate me? The knife is too near the edge:
they'll find it when they're swimming or diving
for snails.

(WADES INTO THE POND)

Ich find's nicht. Aber ich muss mich waschen.
Ich bin blutig. Da ein Fleck—und noch einer.
Weh! Weh! Ich wasche mich mit Blut—das
Wasser ist Blut . . . Blut . . .

I can't find it. But I must wash myself.
There's blood on me. There's a spot here—
and another. Oh, God! I am washing
myself in blood—the water is blood . . . blood . . .

(DROWNS)
(THE DOCTOR APPEARS, FOLLOWED BY THE CAPTAIN.)

CAPTAIN

Halt!

Wait!

DOCTOR *(STOPS)*

Hören Sie? Dort!

Can you hear? There!

CAPTAIN

Jesus! Das war ein Ton!

Jesus! What a ghastly sound!

(STOPS AS WELL)

DOCTOR *(POINTING TO THE POND)*

Ja, dort!

Yes, there!

CAPTAIN

Es ist das Wasser im Teich. Das Wasser ruft.
Es ist schon lange Niemand ertrunken.
Kommen Sie, Doktor!
Es ist nicht gut zu hören.

It's the water in the pond. The water is calling.
It's been a long time since anyone drowned.
Come away, Doctor.
It's not good for us to be hearing it.

(TRIES TO DRAG THE DOCTOR AWAY)

DOCTOR *(RESISTING, AND CONTINUING TO LISTEN)*

Das stöhnt, als stürbe ein Mensch.
Da ertrinkt Jemand!

There's a groan, as though someone were
dying. Somebody's drowning!

CAPTAIN

Unheimlich! Der Mond rot, und die Nebel grau.
Hören Sie? . . . Jetzt wieder das Ächzen.

It's eerie! The moon is red, and the mist is grey.
Can you hear? . . . That moaning again.

DOCTOR

Stiller, . . . jetzt ganz still.

It's getting quieter . . . now it's stopped
altogether.

CAPTAIN

Kommen Sie! Kommen Sie schnell!

Come! Come quickly!

(HE RUSHES OFF, PULLING THE DOCTOR ALONG WITH HIM.)

SCENE CHANGE
INVENTION ON A KEY (D MINOR)

SCENE FIVE
INVENTION ON A QUAVER RHYTHM
IN FRONT OF MARIE'S DOOR. MORNING. BRIGHT SUNSHINE.
(CHILDREN ARE NOISILY AT PLAY. MARIE'S CHILD IS RIDING A HOBBY-HORSE.)

CHILDREN

Ringel, Ringel, Rosenkranz, Ringelreih'n,   Ring-a-ring-a-roses,
Ringel, Ringel, Rosenkranz, Ring . . .   A pocket full of . . .

(THEIR SONG AND GAME ARE INTERRUPTED BY OTHER CHILDREN BURSTING IN.)

ONE OF THE NEWCOMERS

Du, Käthe! Die Marie!   Hey, Katie! Have you heard about Marie?

SECOND CHILD

Was ist?   What's happened?

FIRST CHILD

Weisst' es nit? Sie sind schon Alle 'naus.   Don't you know? They've all gone out there.

THIRD CHILD *(TO MARIE'S LITTLE BOY)*

Du! Dein' Mutter ist tot!   Hey! Your mother's dead!

MARIE'S SON *(STILL RIDING)*

Hopp, hopp! Hopp, hopp! Hopp, hopp!   Hop, hop! Hop, hop! Hop, hop!

SECOND CHILD

Wo ist sie denn?   Where is she, then?

FIRST CHILD

Draus' liegt sie, am Weg, neben dem Teich.   She's lying out there, on the path near the pond.

THIRD CHILD

Kommt, anschaun!   Come and have a look!

(ALL THE CHILDREN RUN OFF.)

MARIE'S SON *(CONTINUING TO RIDE)*

Hopp, hopp! Hopp, hopp! Hopp, hopp!   Hop, hop! Hop, hop! Hop, hop!

(HE HESITATES FOR A MOMENT AND THEN RIDES AFTER THE OTHER CHILDREN.)

END OF THE OPERA
LIBRETTO BY ALBAN BERG, AFTER GEORG BÜCHNER'S PLAY *WOYZECK* (1837)

Translated by Sarah E. Soulsby

33. Sergei Prokofiev

Alexander Nevsky, Seventh Movement (1939)

8CD: 7/ 58 – 61
8Cas: 7B/4

34. Lillian Hardin

Hotter Than That (1927)

8CD: 7/ 70 – 75
8Cas: 7B/7

Head (tune and chord progression)

70 Introduction [not transcribed]

71 Chorus 1, solo cornet [final break not transcribed]

72 Chorus 2 [not transcribed]

Chorus 2, final vocal break

73 Chorus 3

74 75 Choruses 4 and 5 [not transcribed]

chords: I IV I V I

measures: 4 2 2 2 2 } Blues form

35. Duke Ellington

Ko-Ko (1940)

form - 12 bar blues

8CD: 8/ 1 – 8
4CD: 4/ 32 – 39
8Cas: 8A/1
4Cas: 4A/7

36. Aaron Copland	8CD: 8/ 9 – 13
Billy the Kid, Scene 1, *Street in a Frontier Town* (orchestral suite) (1939)	4CD: 4/ ⟨22⟩ – ⟨26⟩ 8Cas: 8A/2 4Cas: 4A/5

INSTRUMENTATION

Piccolo
2 Flutes
2 Oboes
2 Clarinets
2 Bassoons

4 French horns
3 Trumpets
3 Trombones
Tuba

Timpani
Glockenspiel
Xylophone
Tin whistle
Sleigh bells
Wood blocks
Gourd
Snare drum
Slapstick
Cymbals

Bass drum
Triangle

Piano

Violins I, II
Violas
Cellos
Double basses

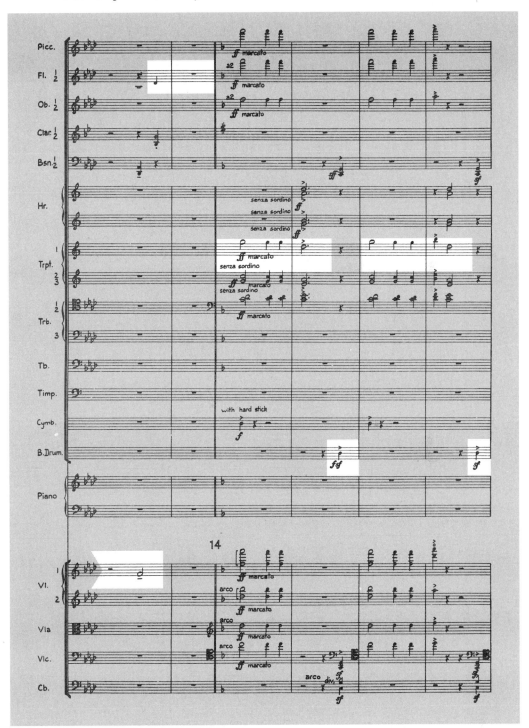

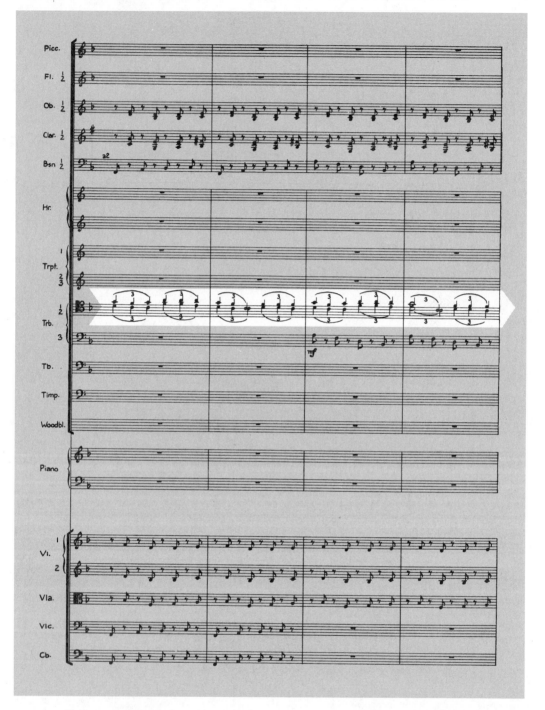

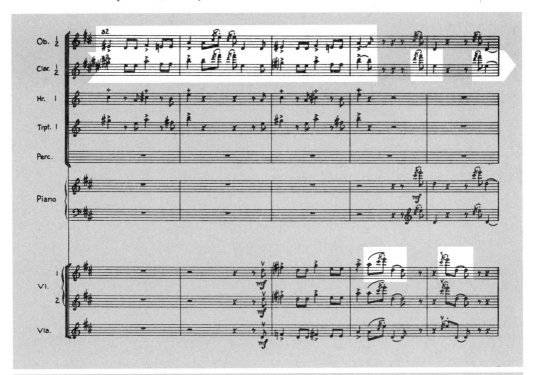

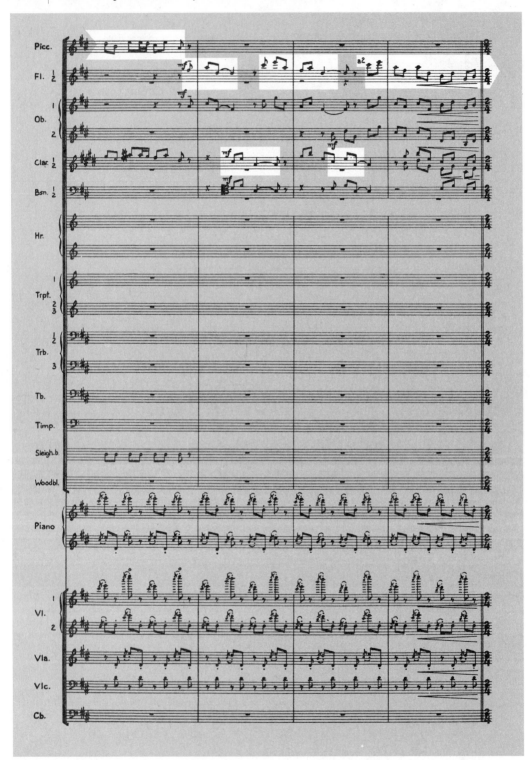

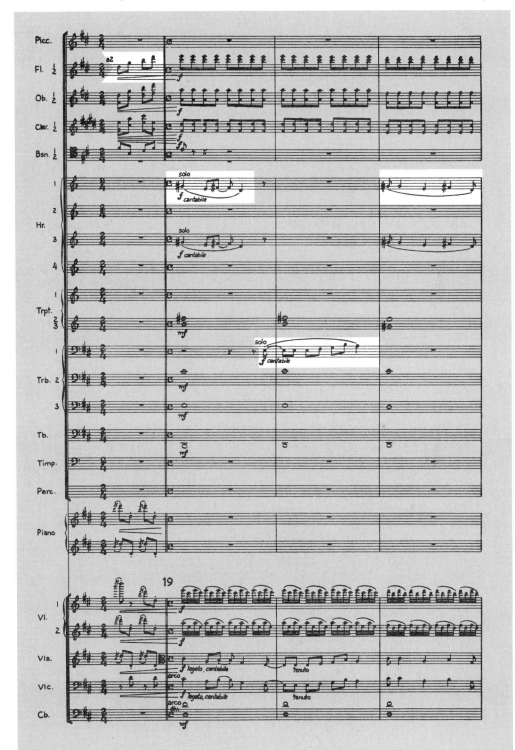

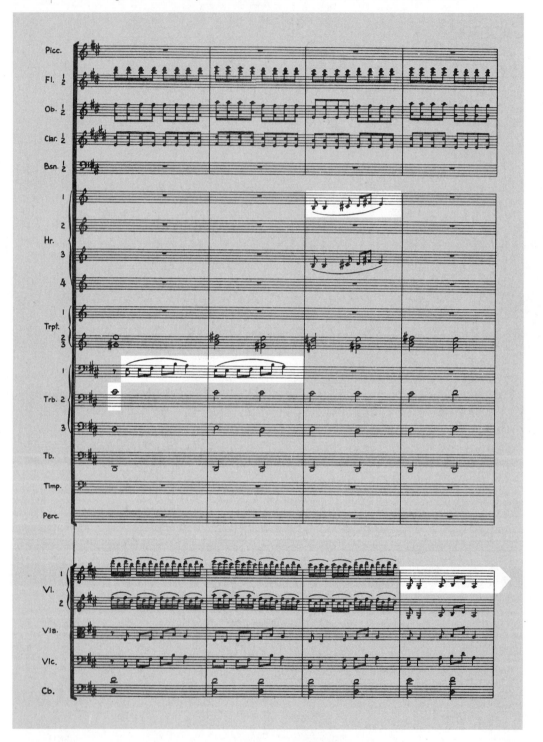

Mexican Dance and Finale

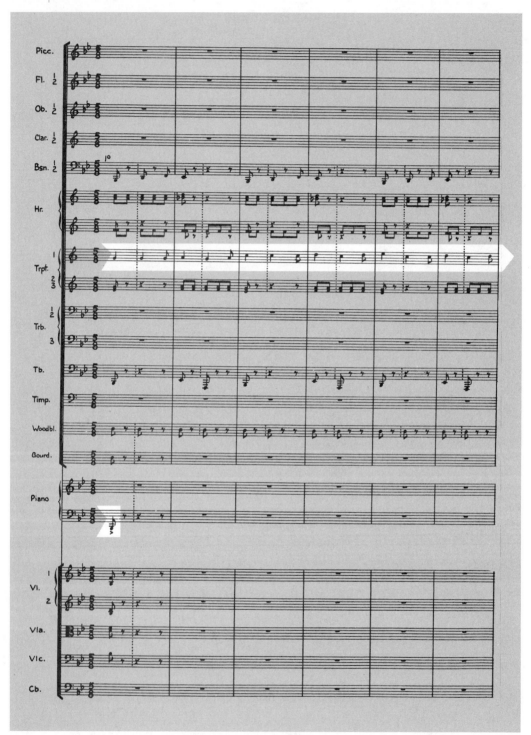

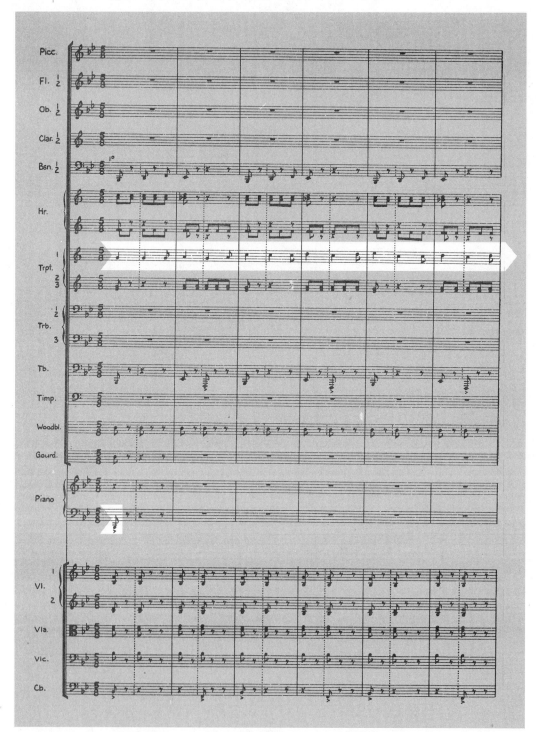

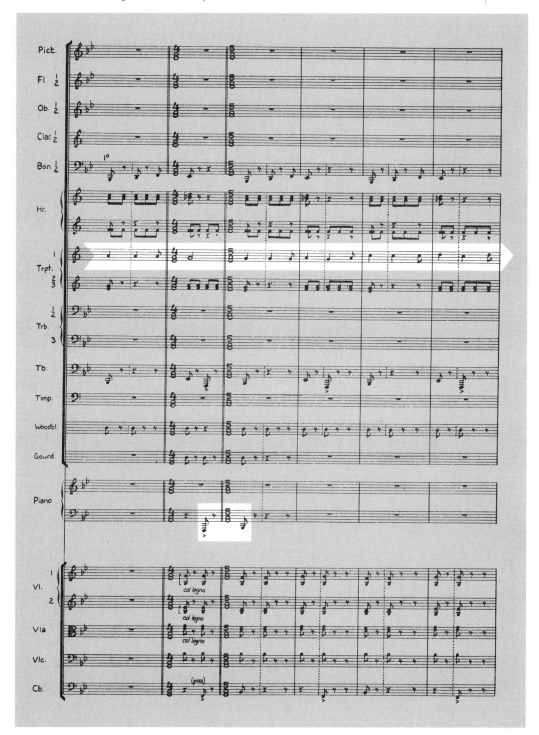

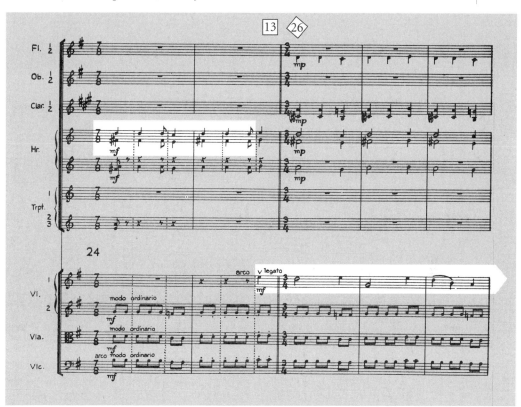

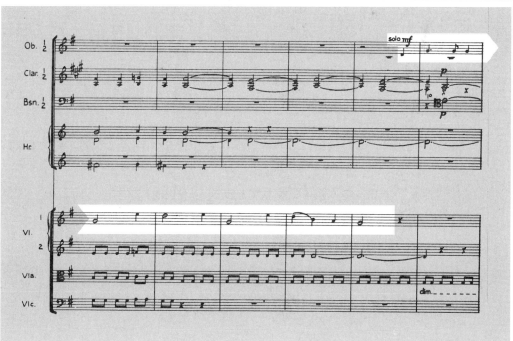

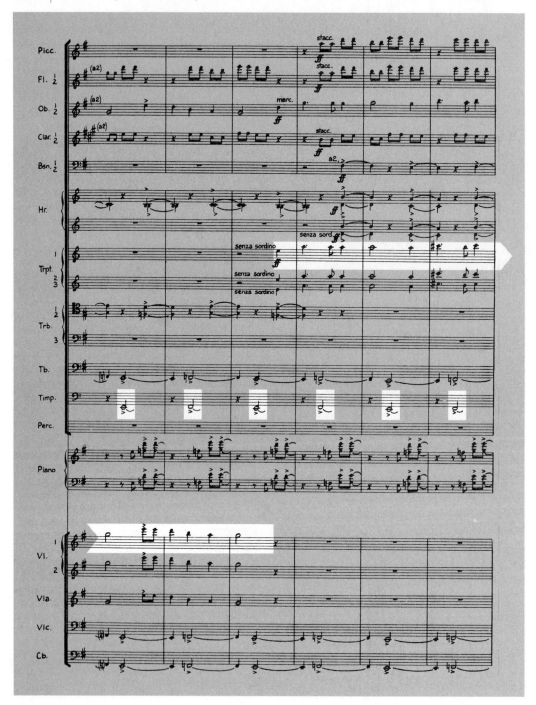

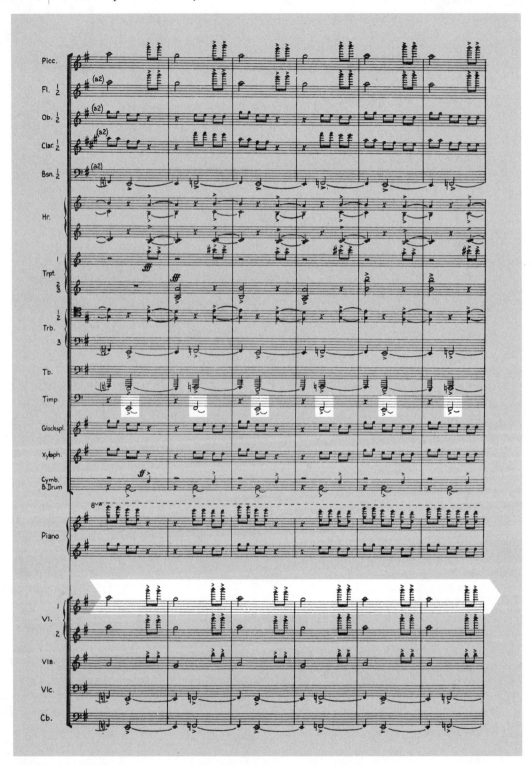

37. Richard Rodgers

My Funny Valentine (1937)

8CD: 7/ 62 – 69
8Cas: 7B/5–6
MasterWorks

Original Version, from *Babes in Arms* (1937)

63 66

va - cant brow and thy tous - led hair con - ceal thy good in - tent. Thou

no - ble, up - right, truth - ful, sin - cere and slight - ly dop - ey gent, you're

Refrain *(slowly, with much expression)*

My fun - ny Val - en - tine, Sweet com - ic

Val - en - tine, You make me smile with my

Gerry Mulligan Quartet Version (1953)

Transcribed by Evan Solot.

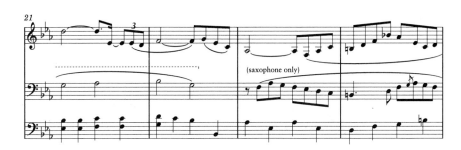

38. Olivier Messiaen

Quatuor pour la fin du temps (Quartet for the End of Time), Second Movement, *Vocalise, pour l'Ange qui annonce la fin du Temps (Vocalise, for the Angel who announces the end of Time)* (1941)

8CD: 8/ 16 – 18
8Cas: 8A/4

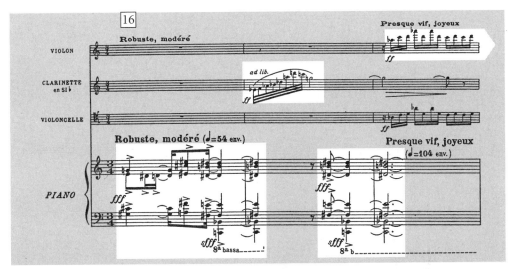

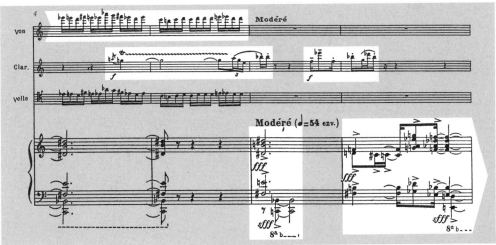

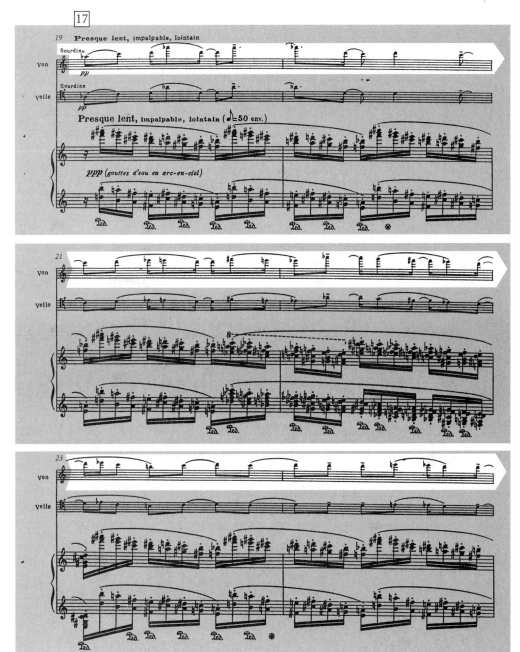

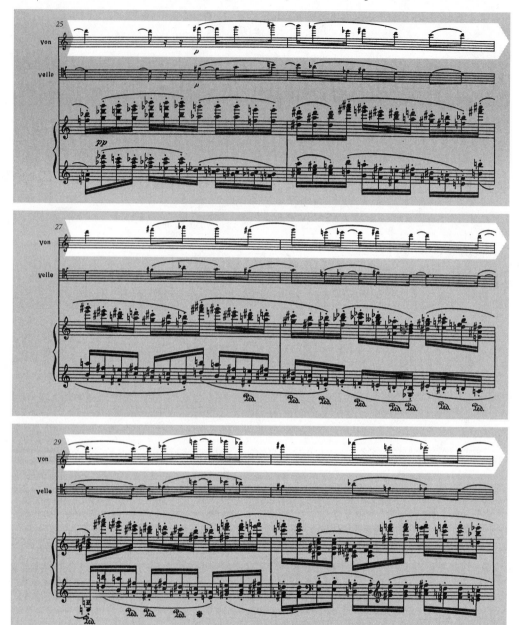

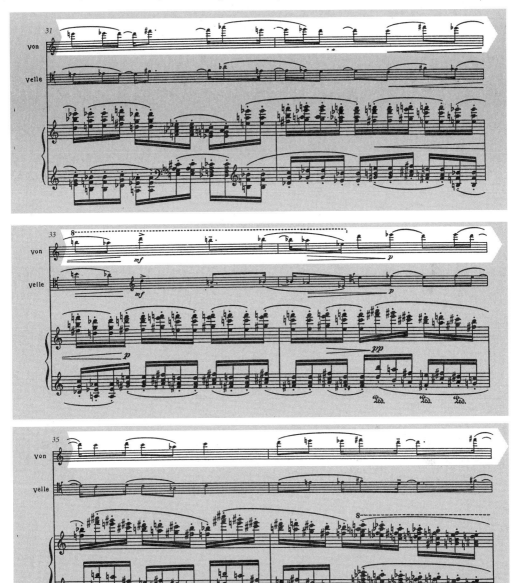

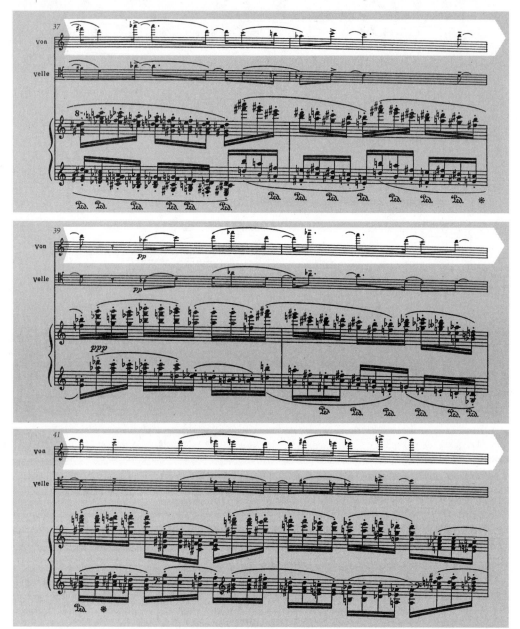

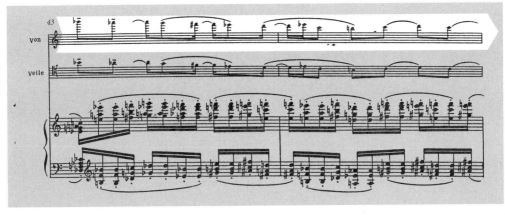

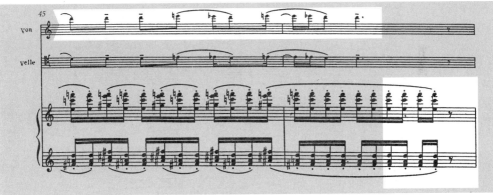

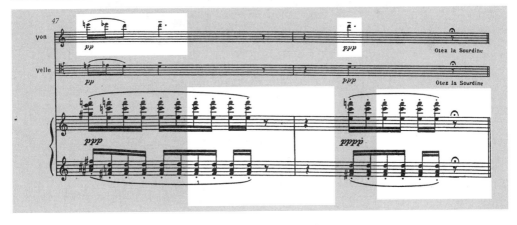

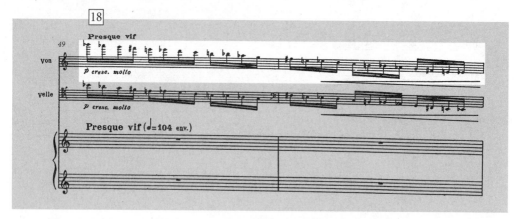

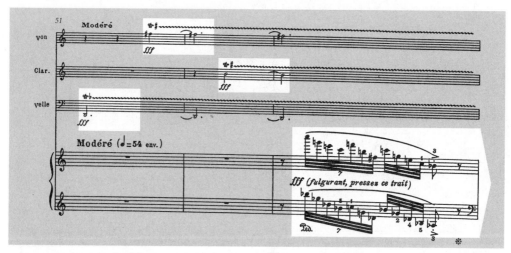

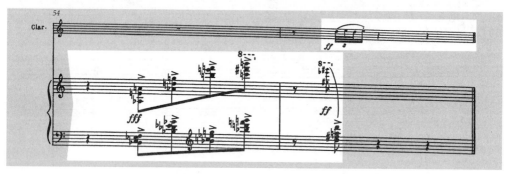

39. Witold Lutosławski

Jeux vénitiens (Venetian Games),
First Movement (1961)

8CD: 8/ 14 – 15
8Cas: 8A/3

Instrumentation

2 flauti (II anche flauto piccolo)
1 oboe
3 clarinetti in si♭ (III anche clarinetto basso in si♭)
1 fagotto

1 tromba in do
1 corno in fa
1 trombone

percussione (4 esecutori)
       I 3 timpani scordati (3 dimensioni)
      II 3 tamburi (soprano, alto, tenore), tamburo rullante
      III xilofono, 3 piatti sospesi (soprano, alto, tenore), tam-tam, 5 tom-tom
      IV claves, vibrafono senza motore

arpa
pianoforte (2 esecutori; II anche celesta)

4 violini
3 viole
3 violoncelli
2 contrabbassi

Duration ca. 13′

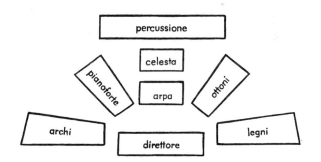

The piccolo, xylophone, and celesta are notated an octave lower, and the double-basses an octave higher, than they sound. All the other instruments are notated at their actual pitch. In this score the signs ♯ and ♭ apply only to the notes they precede. Notes without accidentals should always be read as naturals.

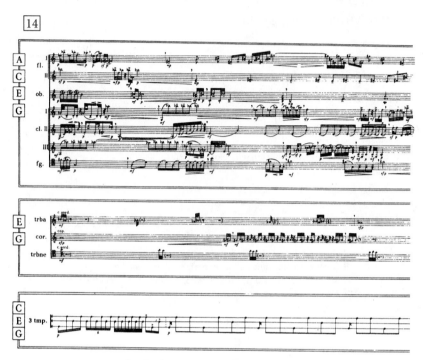

Order of performance: A B C D E F G H

Sections A C E G :

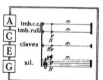

A is played by the woodwinds and percussion group; C by the woodwinds, kettle-drums, and percussion; E by the woodwinds, brass, kettledrums, and percussion; G by the woodwinds, brass, kettledrums, percussion, and piano. The broken "bar lines" with a caesura above call for a caesura of optional length; on the length of the caesura will depend the density of the texture.

Duration of the particular sections: A = 12″, C = 18″, E = 6″, G = 24″. The conductor gives the sign for the beginning and end of each section (the beat showing the end of section A also indicates the beginning of section B, the beat showing the end of C, the beginning of D, etc.). When the sign for the end of each section is given, the performers must interrupt playing immediately. If by this time a player has al-

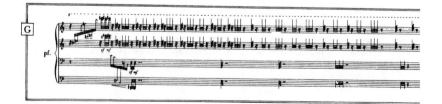

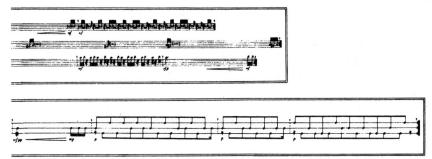

ready played his part to the end, he should repeat it from the beginning of the section. In the following sections, which are indicated by the letters in the order C, E, G, the individual parts ought not to be played from the beginning but from any other phrase between two caesuras. Each musician should play his part with the same freedom as if he were playing it alone; the rhythmic values serve only as a guide, and the basic tempo is between $\flat$ = 140 and $\flat$ = 150.

Sections B D F H:

The bar lines, rhythmical values, and meter are intended merely for orientation: the music should be played with the greatest possible freedom. The number of notes at places like the third bar of section B in the first viola part depends on the strength of the player's bowing (*spiccato* or preferably *ricochet*). In section D the first violin part should be played independently of the conductor and the rest of the ensemble.

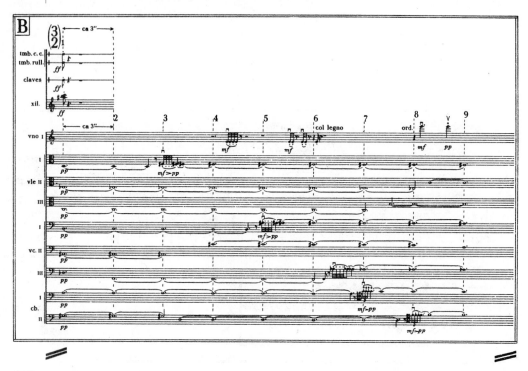

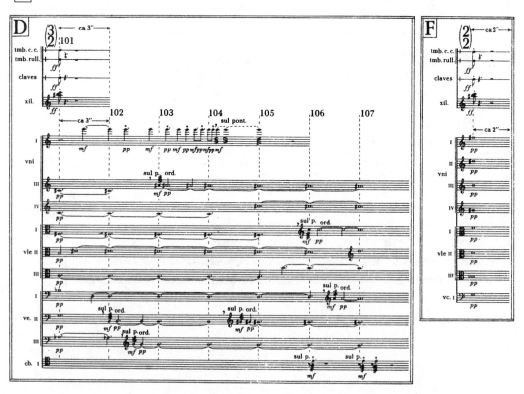

40. Leonard Bernstein *Mambo* and *Tonight* Ensemble, from *West Side Story* (1957)	8CD: 8/ 19 – 29 4CD: 4/ ◇40◇ – ◇50◇ 8Cas: 8A/5–6 4Cas: 4A/8–9

INSTRUMENTATION

WOODWINDS

Most musical theater scores call for woodwind players (called reeds) to double on a variety of instruments. In *Mambo,* five reed books (numbered I–V) appear in different positions in the score, depending on the range of the instrument played (highest on the top line, lowest on the bottom).

Reed I: Alto saxophone
          B-flat clarinet
          Flute

Reed II: E-flat clarinet
          B-flat clarinet

Reed III: B-flat clarinet
          Tenor saxophone
          Flute

Reed IV: Piccolo
         Bass saxophone
         B-flat clarinet
         Flute

Reed V: Bassoon

BRASSES

2 French horns
3 B-flat trumpets
2 Trombones

PERCUSSION

Timpani
Bongos
Timbales
Conga
Pitched drums

Maracas
Cowbells
Guiro
Xylophone
Piano

Trap set:
  Snare drum
  Tenor drum
  Bass drum
  Cymbals

STRINGS

7 Violins
4 Cellos
  Double bass

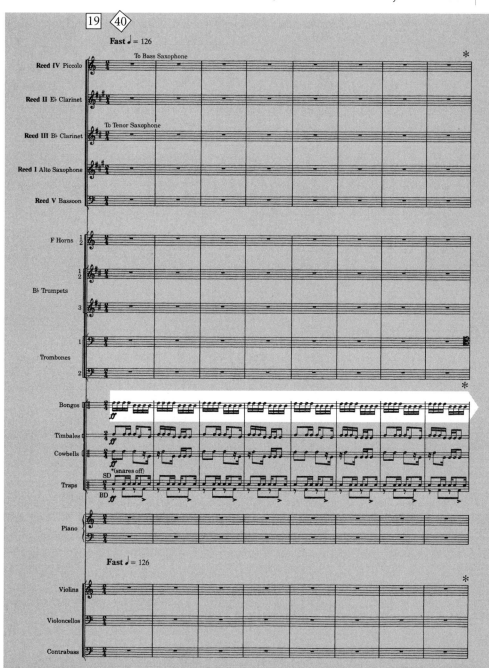

Editor's note: The Norton Recordings performance, which is the original Broadway cast recording, cuts the following five pages and resumes at measure 43 (p. 787).

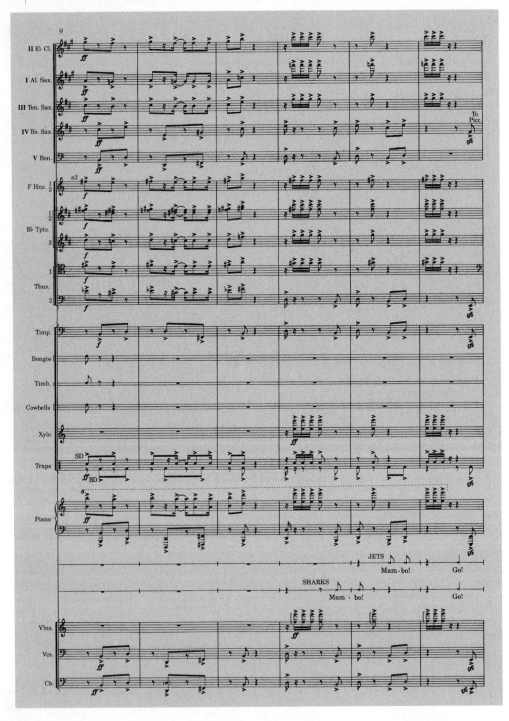

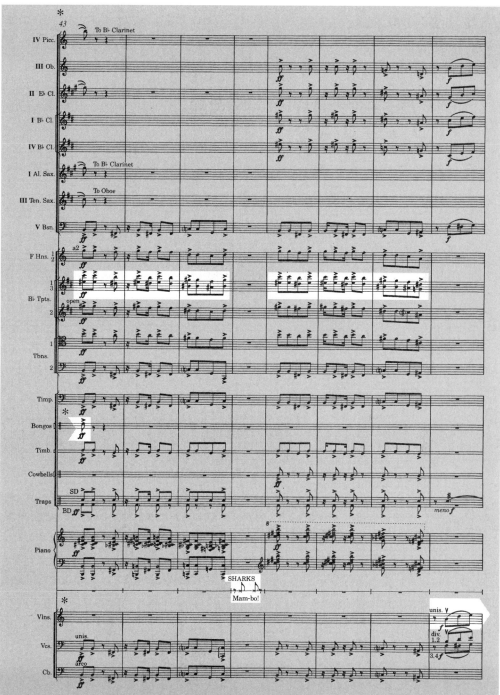

Note: The Norton Recordings performance resumes here.

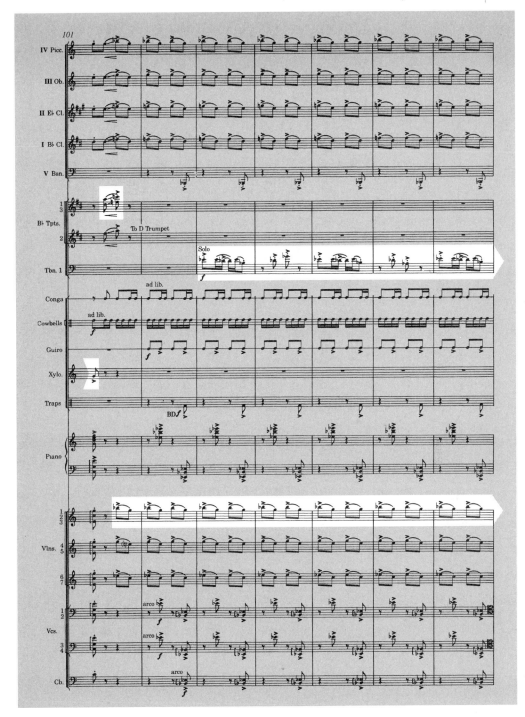

* maracas may be separate player.

(Tony and Maria see each other)

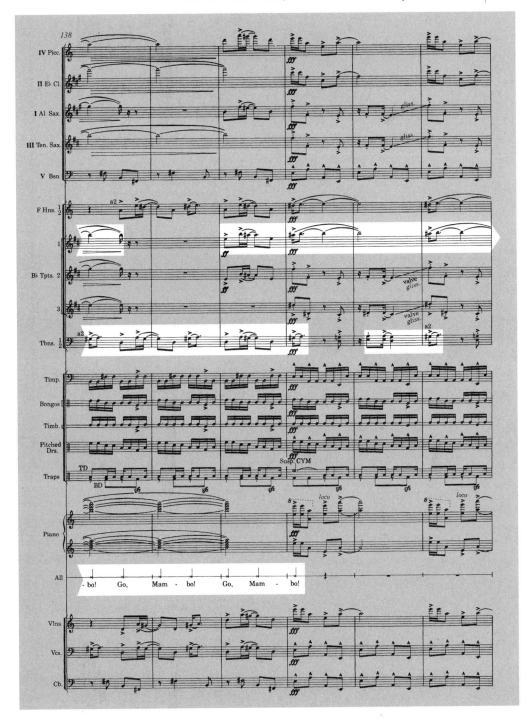

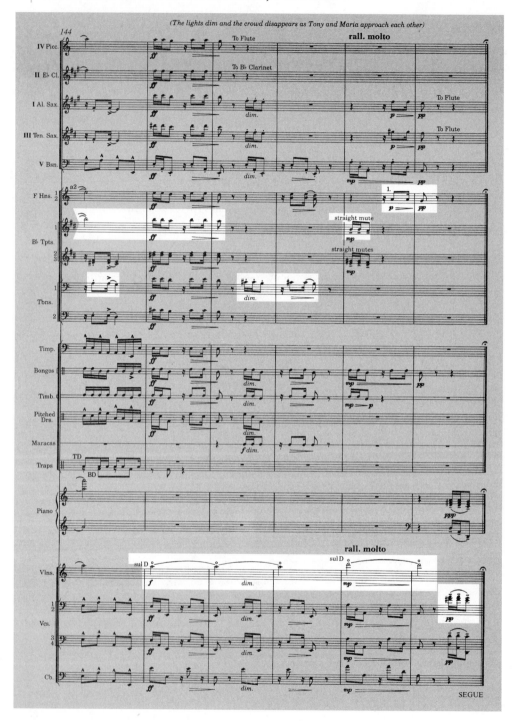

SEGUE

Tonight

Ensemble

Maria, Tony, Anita, Riff, Bernardo*

*If the scene is staged with more than the designated five people, the members of the gangs may sing with their respective leaders.

* The part of Anita may be augmented by voices in the wings from here to the end.

* The part of Maria may be augmented by voices in the wings from here to the end.

41. György Ligeti

Désordre (Disorder), from *Etudes for Piano,* Book I (1985)

8CD: 8/ 30 – 32
4CD: 4/ 64 – 66
8Cas: 8A/7
4Cas: 4B/2

Composer's directions: Use the pedal very discreetly throughout the entire piece.

Editor's note: Measure numbers pertain to left hand.

Composer's directions:

*Dynamic balance: the right hand should play somewhat louder than the left, so that the accented chords in both hands sound equally loud (until the end of the piece).

Gradually add more pedal (but always sparingly).

*Gradual *crescendo* (until the end): the accents gradually become *ff*, then *fff* (with the right hand constantly louder), the eighth notes gradually *mp*, then *mf*.

42. Pierre Boulez

Le marteau sans maître
(The Hammer Without a Master),
Nos. 1, 3, 7 (1953–54; revised 1957)

8CD: 8/ 37 – 39
8Cas: 8A/9–11

1. *Avant "L'artisanat furieux" (Before "Furious Artisans")*

Editor's note: The symbols between the staves are intended for the conductor.

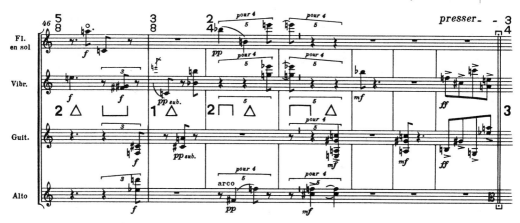

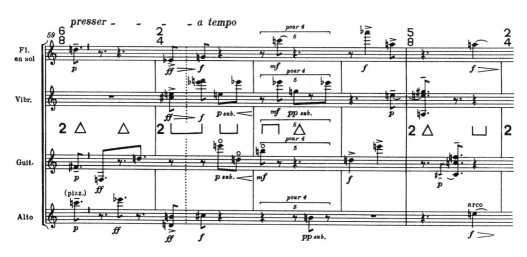

3. *L'artisanat furieux (Furious Artisans)*

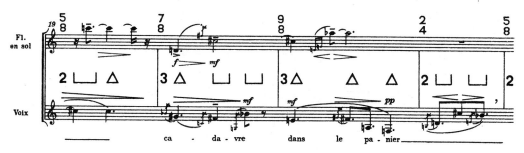

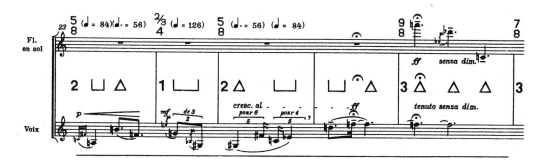

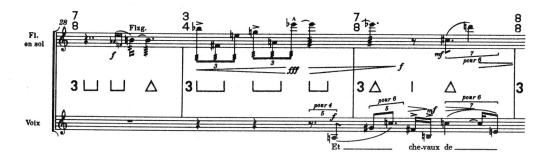

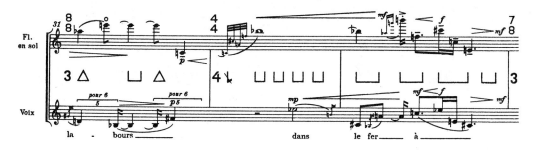

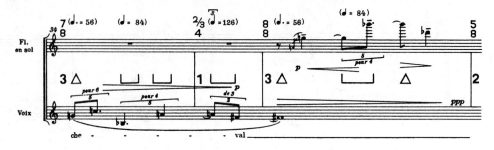

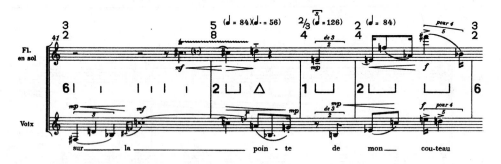

TEXT AND TRANSLATION

La roulotte rouge au bord du clou
Et cadavre dans le panier
Et chevaux de labours dans le fer à cheval
Je rêve la tête sur la pointe de mon couteau le
 Pérou

The red caravan at the prison's edge
And a corpse in the basket
And the work horses in the horseshoe
I dream of Peru with my head on the point of
 my knife

7. *Après "L'artisanat furieux"* (After "Furious Artisans")

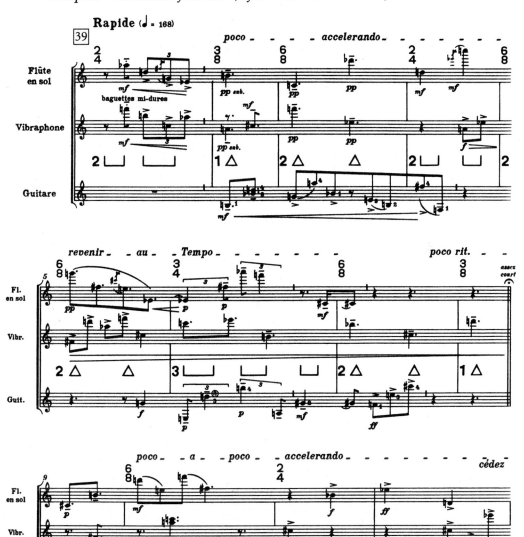

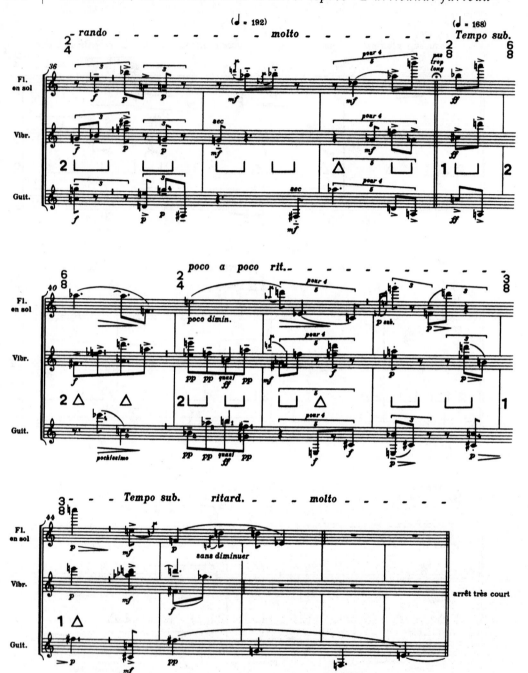

43. George Crumb

Ancient Voices of Children, First Movement,
El niño busca su voz (1970)

8CD: 8/ 40 – 42
4CD: 4/ ⟨61⟩ – ⟨63⟩
8Cas: 8A/12
4Cas: 4B/1

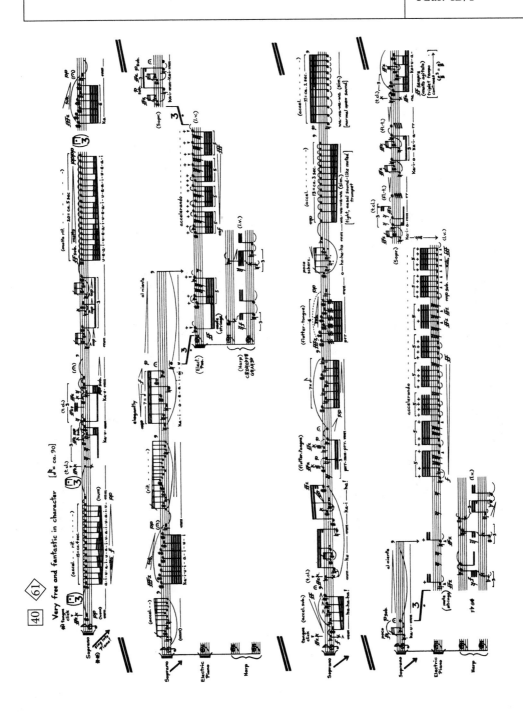

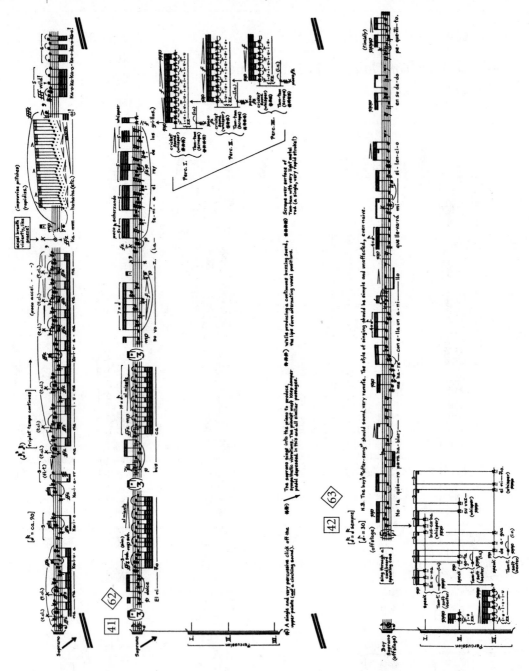

TEXT AND TRANSLATION

El niño busca su voz.
(La tenía el rey de los grillos.)
En una gota de agua
buscaba su voz el niño.

No la quiero para hablar;
me haré con ella un anillo
que llevará mi silencio
en su dedo pequeñito.

The little boy is looking for his voice.
(The king of the crickets had it.)
In a drop of water
the little boy looked for his voice.

I don't want it to speak with;
I will make a ring of it
so that he may wear my silence
on his little finger.

FEDERICO GARCÍA LORCA   *Translated by W. S. Merwin*

44. Steve Reich

City Life, First Movement,
"Check it out" (1995)

8CD: 8/ 43 – 48
4CD: 4/ 84 – 89
8Cas: 8B/1
4Cas: 4B/7

* B♭ Clarinets. Score is written in C.

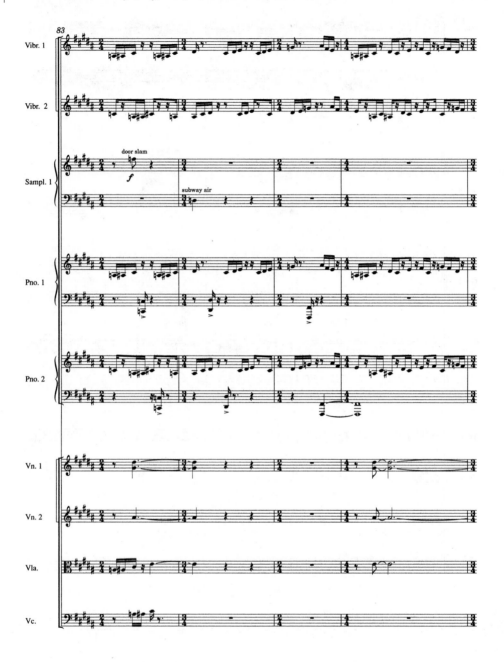

45. Chinary Ung

Spiral, excerpt (1987)

8CD: 8/ 49 – 54
4CD: 4/ ⟨71⟩ – ⟨76⟩
8Cas: 8B/2
4Cas: 4B/4

PERCUSSION INSTRUMENTS

1 glass wind chimes
1 metal wind chimes
1 bell tree
1 sizzle cymbal
4 suspended cymbals
1 gong (med.)
2 tam-tams (high, low)

crotales (two octaves)
tubular bells (small set)
vibraphone
marimba

2 bongos
4 tom-toms
1 bass drum (or very large
    floor tom-tom)

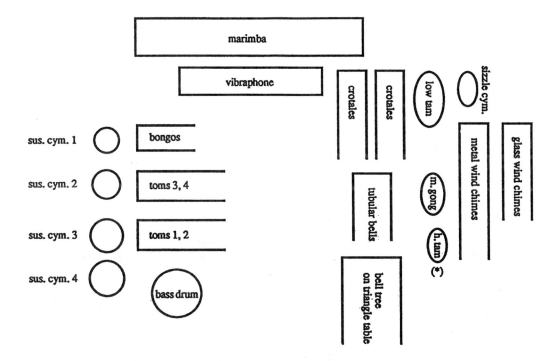

(*) Tam-tams placed on gong stand and suspended over the crotales and tubular bells with the cymbals and wind chimes tucked in behind.

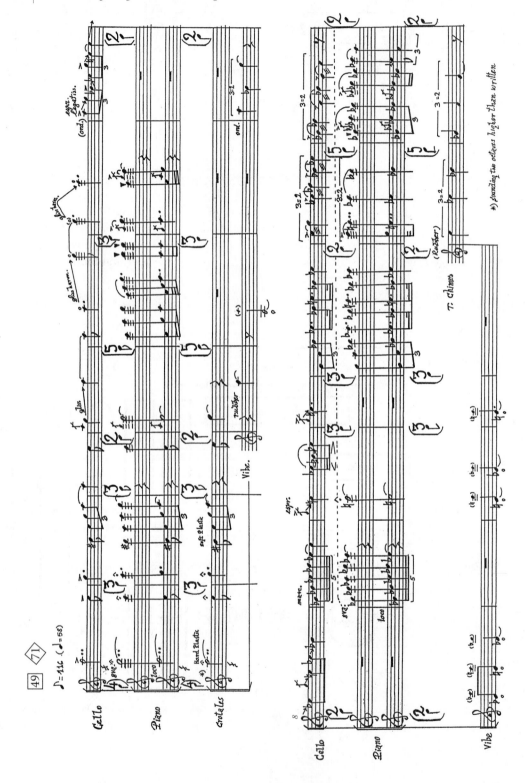

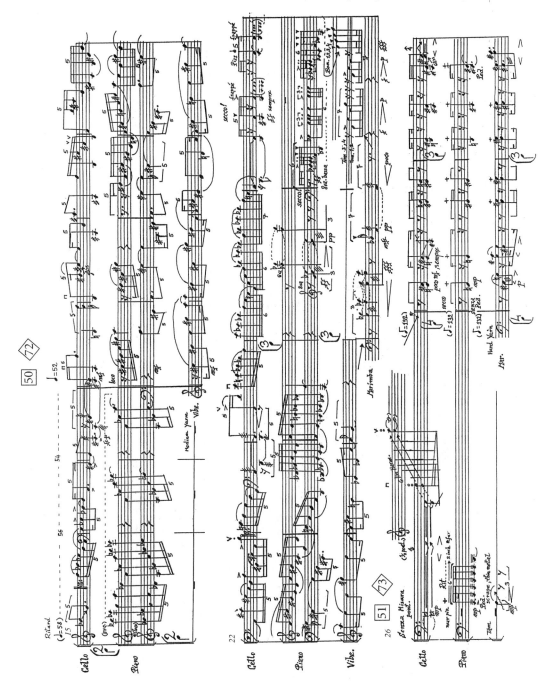

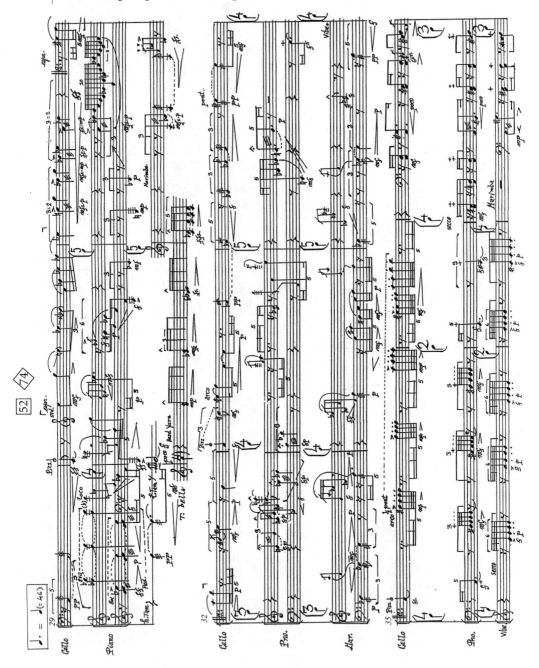

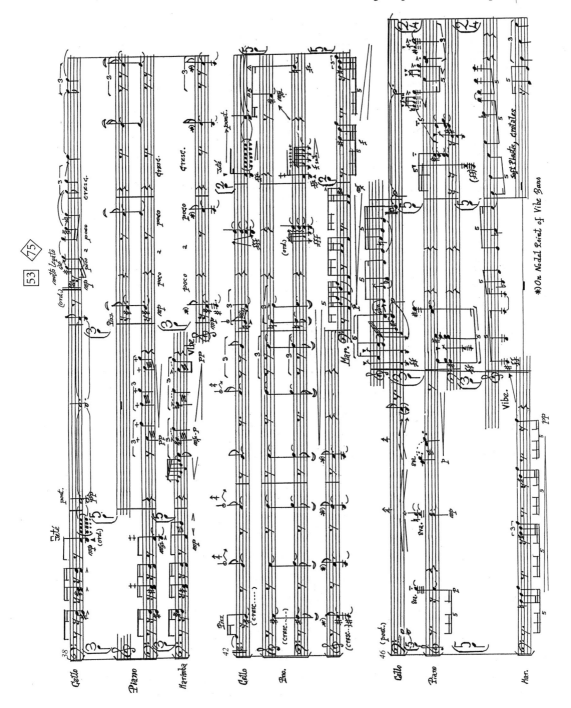

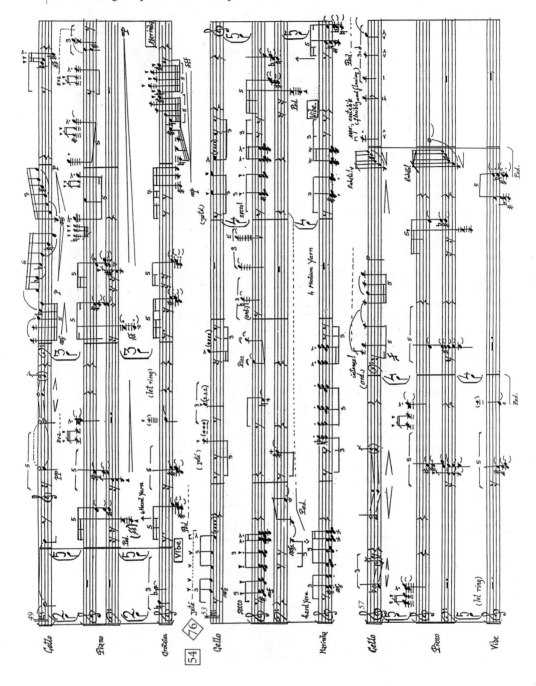

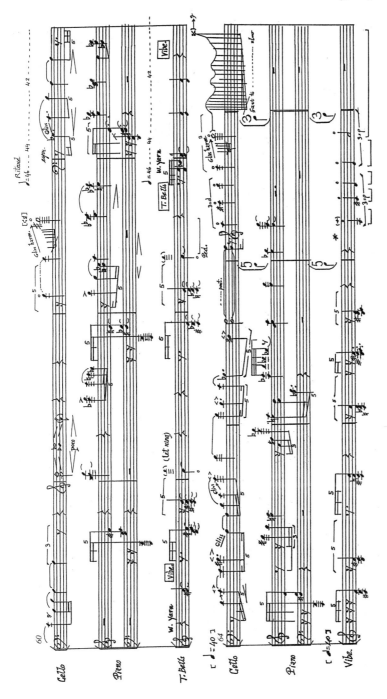

46. Paul Lansky

Notjustmoreidlechatter
(1988)

8CD: 8/ 59 – 62
8Cas: 8B/4

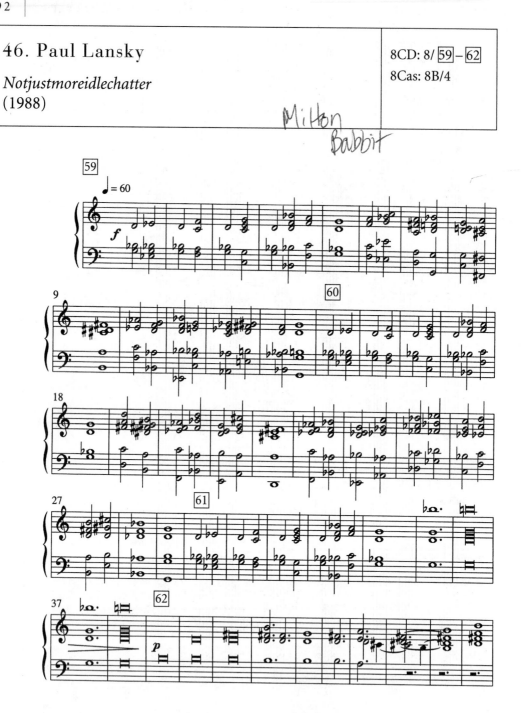

Editor's note: The harmonic outline shown here was kindly prepared by the composer specially for this volume.

*Norton recording fades out here.

47. Libby Larsen

Symphony: Water Music,
First Movement, *Fresh Breeze* (1985)

8CD: 8/ 63 – 65
4CD: 4/ 81 – 83
8Cas: 8B/5
4Cas: 4B/6

Orchestra: Piccolo
2 Flutes
2 Oboes
2 Clarinets, Bb
Bass Clarinet
3 Bassoons

4 Horns, F
3 Trumpets, Bb
3 Trombones
1 Tuba

3 Percussion*

Timpani

Harp

Piano/Celeste

Strings

* Percussion: vibraphone, marimba, orchestra bells, crotales, bell tree,
triangle, wind chimes, tam-tam (large), bass drum,
tenor drum, bongos, tom-toms, snare drum, temple
blocks, tubular bells, sleigh bells, suspended cymbal,
sizzle cymbal, crash cymbals,
wind machine (optional synthesized white or pink noise)

duration: 21' c.

Commissioned by the Minnesota Orchestra under the terms of the
Meet the Composer/Orchestra Residencies Program

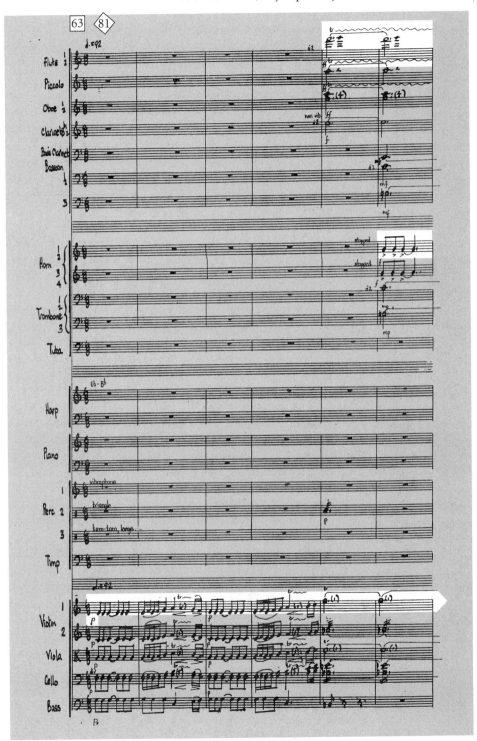

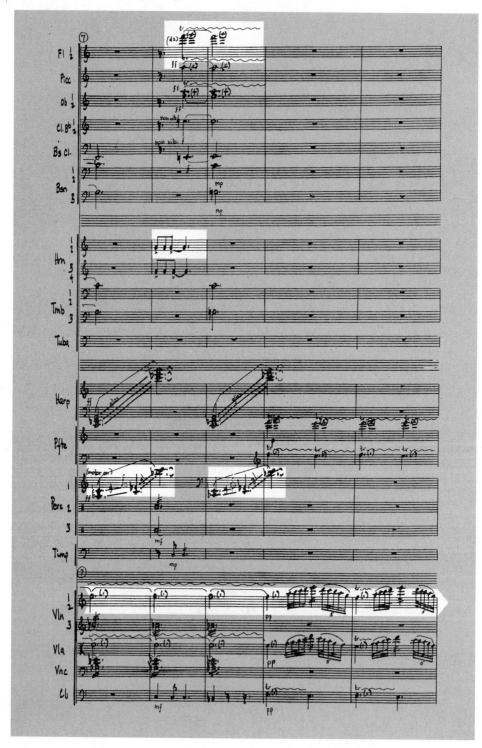

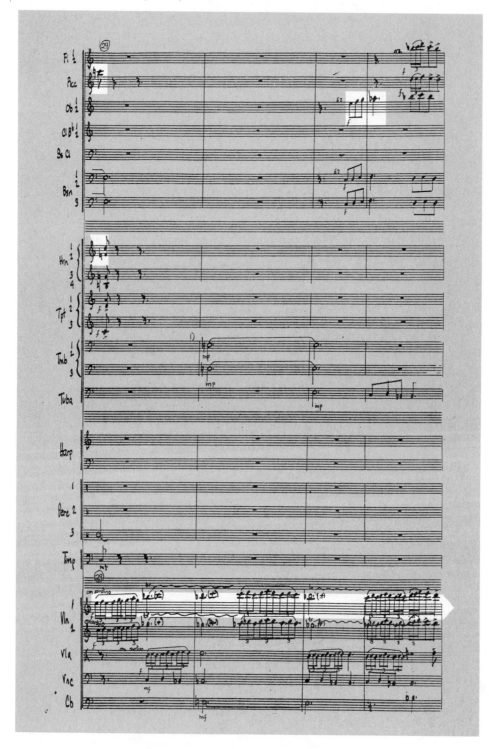

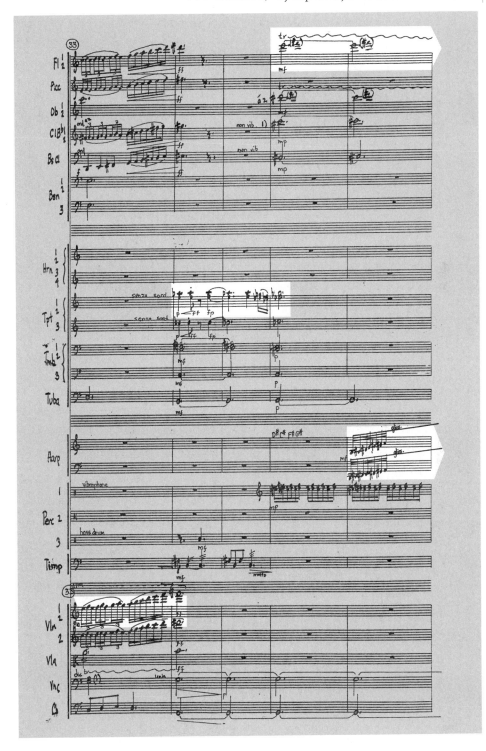

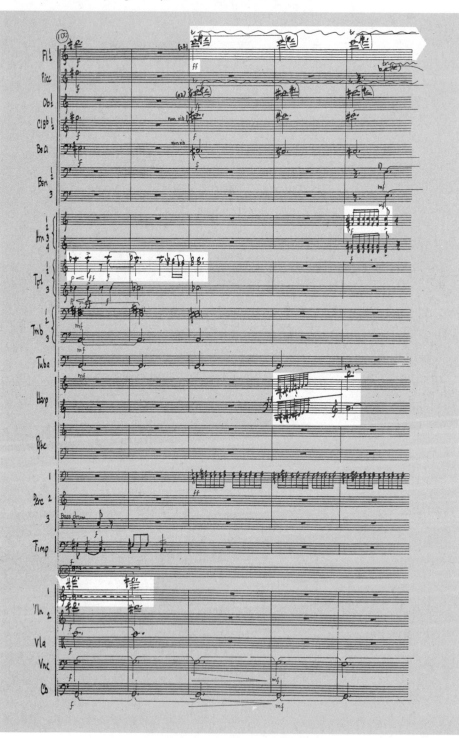

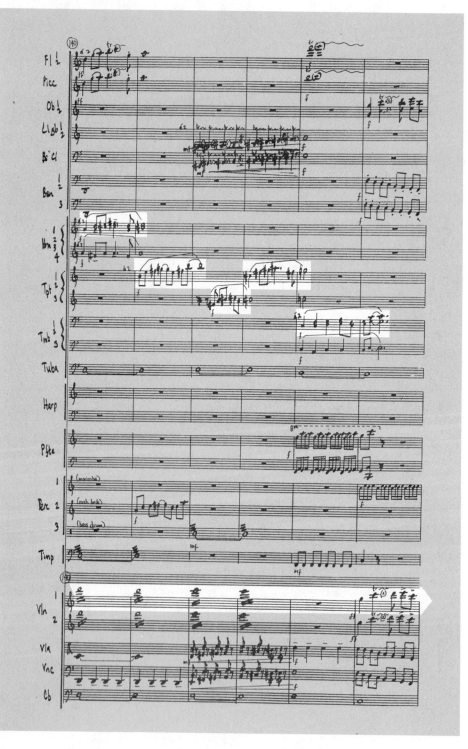

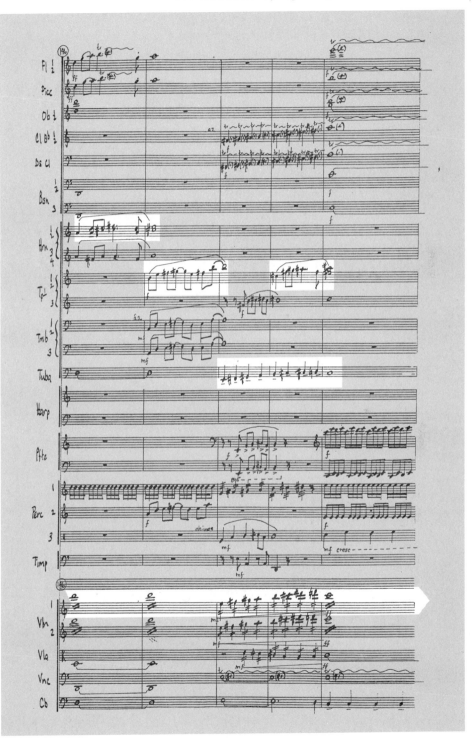

48. Abing (Hua Yanjun)

Er quan ying yue (The Moon Reflected on the Second Springs) (1950)

8CD: 8/ 55 – 58
4CD: 4/ ⟨77⟩ – ⟨80⟩
8Cas: 8B/3
4Cas: 4B/5

55 ⟨77⟩ Statement (Variation) 1

56 ⟨78⟩ Statement (Variation) 2

57 ⟨79⟩ Statement (Variation) 3

58 ⟨80⟩ Statement (Variation) 4

Editor's note: The music above is a notated version of the first statement of the melody as heard on the Norton recording; the following three statements represent elaborations or variations on the same melody.

49. Irish Traditional Dances

The Wind That Shakes the Barley/
The Reel with the Beryle

8CD: 8/ 66 – 75
4CD: 4/ 51 – 60
8Cas: 8B/6
4Cas: 4A/10

66 51 – 70 55   Reel 1

71 56 – 75 60   Reel 2

Editor's note: On the Norton recording, each reel is played five times, with varied instrumentation and embellishments.

Appendix A

Reading a Musical Score

CLEFS

The music for some instruments is written in clefs other than the familiar treble and bass. In the following example, middle C is shown in the four clefs used in orchestral scores:

The *alto clef* is primarily used in viola parts. The *tenor clef* is employed for cello, bassoon, and trombone parts when these instruments play in a high register.

TRANSPOSING INSTRUMENTS

The music for some instruments is customarily written at a pitch different from its actual sound. The following list, with examples, shows the main transposing instruments and the degree of transposition. (In some modern works—such as the Stravinsky example included in volume two of this anthology—all instruments are written at their sounding pitch.)

Instrument	Transposition	Written note	Actual sound
Piccolo Celesta	sounds an octave higher than written		
Trumpet in F	sounds a fourth higher than written		
Trumpet in E	sounds a major third higher than written		
Clarinet in E♭ Trumpet in E♭	sounds a minor third higher than written		
Trumpet in D Clarinet in D	sounds a major second higher than written		
Clarinet in B♭ Trumpet in B♭ Cornet in B♭ French horn in B♭, alto	sounds a major second lower than written		
Clarinet in A Trumpet in A Cornet in A	sounds a minor third lower than written		
French horn in G Alto flute	sounds a fourth lower than written		
English horn French horn in F	sounds a fifth lower than written		
French horn in E	sounds a minor sixth lower than written		
French horn in E♭ Alto saxophone	sounds a major sixth lower than written		
French horn in D	sounds a minor seventh lower than written		
Contrabassoon French horn in C Double bass	sounds an octave lower than written		
Bass clarinet in B♭ Tenor saxophone (written in treble clef) French horn in B♭, bass	sounds a major ninth lower than written		
Tenor saxophone (written in bass clef)	sounds a major second lower than written		
Bass clarinet in A (written in treble clef)	sounds a minor tenth lower than written		
Bass clarinet in A (written in bass clef)	sounds a minor third lower than written		
Baritone saxophone in E♭ (written in treble clef)	sounds an octave and a major sixth lower than written		
Bass saxophone in B♭	sounds two octaves and a major second lower than written		

Appendix B

Instrumental Names and Abbreviations

The following tables set forth the English, Italian, German, and French names used for the various musical instruments in these scores, and their respective abbreviations (when used). Latin voice designations and a table of the foreign-language names for scale degrees and modes are also provided.

English	Italian	German	French
WOODWINDS			
Piccolo (Picc.)	Flauto piccolo (Fl. Picc.)	Kleine Flöte (Kl. Fl.)	Petite flûte
Flute (Fl.)	Flauto (Fl.); Flauto grande (Fl. gr.)	Flöte, Grosse Flöte (Gr. Fl.)	Flûte (Fl.)
Alto flute	Flauto contralto (fl. c-alto)	Altflöte	Flûte en sol
Oboe (Ob.)	Oboe (Ob.)	Hoboe (Hb.); Oboe (Ob.)	Hautbois (Hb.)
English horn (E. H.)	Corno inglese (C. or Cor. ingl., C.i.)	Englisches Horn (E. H.)	Cor anglais (C. A.)
E♭ clarinet	Clarinetto piccolo (clar. picc.)		

English	Italian	German	French
Clarinet (C., Cl., Clt., Clar.)	Clarinetto (Cl., Clar.)	Klarinette (Kl.)	Clarinette (Cl.)
Bass clarinet (B. Cl.)	Clarinetto basso (Cl. b., Cl. basso, Clar. basso)	Bass Klarinette (Bkl.)	Clarinette basse (Cl. bs.)
Bassoon (Bsn., Bssn.)	Fagotto (Fag., Fg.)	Fagott (Fag., Fg.)	Basson (Bssn.)
Contrabassoon (C. Bsn.)	Contrafagotto (Cfg., C. Fag., Cont. F.)	Kontrafagott (Kfg.)	Contrebasson (C. bssn.)
Alto saxophone Tenor saxophone Baritone saxophone	Sassofone	Saxophon	Saxophone
Sarrusophone	Sarrusofano	Sarrusophon	Sarrusophone

<table>
<tr><td colspan="4" align="center">BRASS</td></tr>
</table>

English	Italian	German	French
French horn (Hr., Hn.)	Corno (Cor., C.)	Horn (Hr.) [pl. Hörner (Hrn.)]	Cor; Cor à pistons
Trumpet (Tpt., Trpt., Trp., Tr.)	Tromba (Tr) [pl. Tbe.]	Trompete (Tr., Trp.)	Trompette (Tr.)
Trumpet in D	Tromba piccola (Tr. picc.)		
Cornet	Cornetta	Kornett	Cornet à pistons (C. à p., Pist.)
Trombone (Tr., Tbe., Trb., Trm., Trbe.)	Trombone [pl. Tromboni (Tbni., Trni.)]	Posaune (Ps., Pos.)	Trombone (Tr.)
Bass trombone Tuba (Tb.)	Tuba (Tb., Tba.)	Tuba (Tb.) [also Basstuba (Btb.)]	Tuba (Tb.)
Ophicleide	Oficleide	Ophikleide	Ophicléide

<table>
<tr><td colspan="4" align="center">PERCUSSION</td></tr>
</table>

English	Italian	German	French
Percussion (Perc.)	Percussione	Schlagzeug (Schlag.)	Batterie (Batt.)
Kettledrums (K. D.)	Timpani (Timp., Tp.)	Pauken (Pk.)	Timbales (Timb.)
Snare drum (S. D.)	Tamburo piccolo (Tamb. picc.) Tamburo militare (Tamb. milit.)	Kleine Trommel (Kl. Tr.)	Caisse claire (C. cl.); Caisse roulante Tambour militaire (Tamb. milit.)
Bass drum (B. drum)	Gran cassa (Gr. Cassa, Gr. C., G. C.) Gran tamburo (Gr. Tamb.)	Grosse Trommel (Gr. Tr.)	Grosse caisse (Gr. c.)
Cymbals (Cym., Cymb.) Tam-Tam (Tam.-T.)	Piatti (P., Ptti., Piat.), Cinelli	Becken (Beck.)	Cymbales (Cym.)

English	Italian	German	French
Tambourine (Tamb.)	Tamburino (Tamb.)	Schellentrommel; Tamburin	Tambour de Basque (T. de B., Tamb. de Basque)
Triangle (Trgl., Tri.)	Triangolo (Trgl.)	Triangel	Triangle (Triang.)
Glockenspiel (Glocken.)	Campanelli (Cmp.)	Glockenspiel	Carillon
Bells; chimes, tubular bells, orchestral bells	Campane (Cmp.)	Glocken	Cloches
Antique cymbals	Crotali; Piatti antichi	Antike Zimbeln	Crotales; Cymbales antiques
Sleigh bells	Sonagli (Son.)	Schellen	Grelots
Xylophone (Xyl.)	Xilofono	Xylophon	Xylophone
Cowbells		Herdenglocken	
Crash cymbal			Grande cymbale chinoise
Siren			Sirène
Lion's roar			Tambour à corde
Slapstick			Fouet
Wood blocks			Blocs chinois
Castanet	Castagnette, macchere	Kastagnette	Castagnette
Bongos			
Bell tree			
Tom tom			
Conga			
Guiro			

STRINGS			
Violin (V., Vl., Vln., Vi., Vn.)	Violino (V., Vl., Vln.)	Violine (V., Vl., Vln.); Geige (Gg.)	Violon (V., Vl., Vln.)
Viola (Va., Vl.) [pl. Vas.]	Viola (Va., Vla.) [pl. Viole (Vle.)]	Bratsche (Br.)	Alto (A.)
Violoncello; Cello (Vcl., Vc.)	Violoncello (Vc., Vlc., Vcllo.)	Violoncell (Vc., Vlc.)	Violoncelle (Vc.)
Double bass (D. Bs.)	Contrabasso (Cb., C. B.) [pl. Contrabassi or Bassi (C. Bassi, Bi.)]	Kontrabass (Kb.)	Contrebasse (C. B.)

OTHER INSTRUMENTS			
Harp (Hp., Hrp.)	Arpa (A., Arp.)	Harfe (Hrf.)	Harpe (Hp.)
Piano	Pianoforte (P.-f., Pft.)	Klavier	Piano

English	Italian	German	French
Celesta (Cel.)	Celesta	Celesta	Célesta
Harpsichord	Cembalo	Cembalo	Clavecin
Harmonium (Harmon.)			
Organ (Org.)	Organo	Orgel	Orgue
Guitar		Gitarre (Git.)	
Mandoline (Mand.)			
Marimba			
Vibraphone			
Sampler			
Uillean pipe			
Bodhran			
Concertina			
Tin whistle, penny whistle			
Erhu			
Yangqin			

Voice Designations

English	German
Soprano (S)	Sopran
Alto (A)	Alt
Tenor (T)	Tenor
Bass (B)	Bass
Voice	Singstimme
Voice in Sprechstimme	Rezitation
Chorus	Chor

Names of Scale Degrees and Modes

English	Italian	German	French
SCALE DEGREES			
C C-sharp	do do diesis	C Cis	ut ut dièse
D-flat D D-sharp	re bemolle re re diesis	Des D Dis	ré bémol ré ré dièse
E-flat E E-sharp	mi bemolle mi mi diesis	Es E Eis	mi bémol mi mi dièse
F-flat F F-sharp	fa bemolle fa fa diesis	Fes F Fis	fa bémol fa fa dièse
G-flat G G-sharp	sol bemolle sol sol diesis	Ges G Gis	sol bémol sol sol dièse
A-flat A A-sharp	la bemolle la la diesis	As A Ais	la bémol la la dièse
B-flat B B-sharp	si bemolle si si diesis	B H His	si bémol si si dièse
C-flat	do bemolle	Ces	ut bémol
MODES			
major minor	maggiore minore	dur moll	majeur mineur

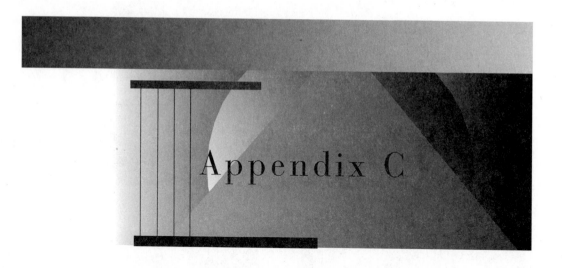

Appendix C

Glossary of Musical Terms Used in the Scores

The following glossary is not intended to be a complete dictionary of musical terms, nor is knowledge of all these terms necessary to follow the scores in this book. However, as listeners gain experience in following scores, they will find it useful and interesting to understand the composer's directions with regard to tempo, dynamics, and methods of performance.

In most cases, compound terms have been broken down and defined separately, as they often recur in varying combinations. A few common foreign-language particles are included in addition to the musical terms. Note that names and abbreviations for instruments and for scale degrees will be found in Appendix B.

a The phrases *a 2, a 3* (etc.) indicate the number of parts to be played by 2, 3 (etc.) players; when a simple number (1, 2, etc.) is placed over a part, it indicates that only the first (second, etc.) player in that group should play.

ab Off.

aber But.

accelerando (accel.) Growing faster.

accentato, accentué Accented.

accompagnando Accompanying.

accompagnemento Accompaniment.

accordato, accordez Tune the instrument as specified.

adagio Slow, leisurely.

affettuoso With emotion.

affrettare (affrett.) Hastening a little.

agitando, agitato Agitated, excited.

al fine "The end"; an indication to return to the start of a piece and to repeat it only to the point marked "fine."

alla breve Indicates two beats to a measure, at a rather quick tempo.

allargando (allarg.) Growing broader.

alle, alles All, every, each.

allegretto A moderately fast tempo (between allegro and andante).

allegrezza Gaiety.

allegro A rapid tempo (between allegretto and presto).

allein Alone, solo.

allmählich Gradually (*allmählich wieder gleich mässig fliessend werden*, gradually becoming even-flowing again).

alta, alto, altus (A.) The deeper of the two main divisions of women's (or boys') voices.

am Steg On the bridge (of a string instrument).

ancora Again.

andante A moderately slow tempo (between adagio and allegretto).

andantino A moderately slow tempo.

Anfang Beginning, initial.

anima Spirit, animation.

animando With increasing animation.

animant, animato, animé, animez Animated.

aperto Indicates open notes on the horn, open strings, and undamped piano notes.

a piacere The execution of the passage is left to the performer's discretion.

appassionato Impassioned.

appena Scarcely, hardly.

apprensivo Apprehensive.

archet Bow.

archi, arco Played with the bow.

arditamente Boldly.

arpeggiando, arpeggiato (arpegg.) Played in harp style, i.e., the notes of the chord played in quick succession rather than simultaneously.

arrêt Break (as in *arrêt long*, long break).

articulato Articulated, separated.

assai Very.

assez Fairly, rather.

attacca Begin what follows without pausing.

a tempo At the original tempo.

auf dem On the (as in *auf dem G*, on the G string).

Ausdruck Expression.

ausdrucksvoll With expression.

äusserst Extreme, utmost.

avec With.

bachetta, bachetti Drumsticks (*bachetti di spugna*, sponge-headed drumsticks).

baguettes Drumsticks (*baguettes de bois*, wooden drumsticks; *baguettes d'éponge*, sponge-headed drumsticks; *baguettes dures*, hard mallets; *baguettes midures*, medium-hard mallets or drumsticks.

bass, bassi, basso, bassus (B.) The lowest male voice.

battere, battuta, battuto (batt.) To beat.

beaucoup A lot.

Becken Cymbals.

bedeutend bewegter With significantly more movement.

behaglich heiter Pleasingly serene or cheerful.

beider Hände With both hands.

ben Very.

bewegt Agitated.

bewegter More agitated.

bisbigliando, bispiglando (bis.) Whispering.

bis zum Schluss dieser Szene To the end of this scene.

blasen Blow.

Blech Brass instruments.

bogen (bog.) Played with the bow.

bois Woodwind.

bouché Muted.

break A jazz term for a short, improvised solo without accompaniment that "breaks" an ensemble passage or introduces an extended solo.

breit Broadly.

breiter More broadly.

brilliante Brilliant.

brio Spirit, vivacity.

burden Refrain.

cadenza (cad., cadenz.) An extended passage for solo instrument in free, improvisatory style.

calando (cal.) Diminishing in volume and speed.

calma, calmo Calm, calmly.

cantabile (cant.) In a singing style.

cantando In a singing manner.

canto Voice (as in *col canto*, a direction for the accompaniment to follow the solo part in tempo and expression).

cantus An older designation for the highest part in a vocal work.

capriccio Capriciously, whimsically.

cedendo Yielding.

cédez Slow down.

changez Change (usually an instruction to retune a string or an instrument).

chiuso See *gestopft*.

chorus In jazz, a single statement of the melodic-harmonic pattern (e.g., 12-bar blues).

chromatisch Chromatic.

circa (ca.) About, approximately.

coda The last part of a piece.

col, colla, colle, coll' With the.

colore Colored.

come prima, come sopra As at first, as previously.

commodo Comfortable, easy.

con With.

corda String; for example, *seconda (2a) corda* is the second string (the A string on the violin).

corto Short, brief.

court Short.

crescendo (cres.) An increase in volume.

cuivré Played with a harsh, blaring tone.

cupa, cupo Gloomy, somber.

da capo (D.C.) Repeat from the beginning.

dal segno (D.S.) Repeat from the sign.

Dämpfer (dpf.) Mutes.

dazu In addition to that, for that purpose.

de, des, die Of, from.

début Beginning.

deciso Determined, resolute.

declamando In a declamatory style.

decrescendo (decresc., decr.) A decreasing of volume.

dehors Outside.

delicato Delicate, delicately.

dem To the.

détaché With a broad, vigorous bow stroke, each note bowed singly.

deutlich Distinctly.

d'exécution Performance.

diminuendo, diminuer (dim., dimin.) A decreasing of volume.

distinto Distinct, clear.

divisés, divisi (div.) Divided; indicates that the instrumental group should be divided into two parts to play the passage in question.

dolce Sweetly and softly.

dolcemente Sweetly.

dolcissimo (dolciss.) Very sweetly.

dolore, doloroso With sorrow.

Doppelgriff Double stop.

doux Sweetly.

drammatico Dramatic.

drängend Pressing on.

dreifach Triple.

dreitaktig Three beats to a measure.

dur Major, as in *G dur* (G major).

durée Duration.

e, et And.

eilen To hurry.

ein One, a.

elegante Elegant, graceful.

Empfindung Feeling.

energico Energetically.

espansione Expansion, broadening.

espressione With expression.

espressivo (espr., espress.) Expressively.

étouffez Muted, dampened.

etwas Somewhat, rather.

expressif Expressively.

facile Simple.

falsetto Male voice singing above normal range, with light sound.

feroce Fierce, ferocious.

fin, fine End, close.

Flatterzunge (Flzg.), flutter-tongue A special tonguing technique for wind instruments, producing a rapid, trill-like sound.

flebile Feeble, plaintive, mournful.

fliessend Flowing.

forte (f) Loud.

fortepiano (fp) Loud, then soft immediately.

fortissimo (ff) Very loud (*fff* indicates a still louder dynamic).

forza Force.

forzando (fz) Forcing, strongly accented.

forzandissimo (ffz) Very strongly accented.

fou Frantic.

frappez To strike.

frei Freely.

freihäng., freihängendes Hanging freely. An indication to the percussionist to let the cymbals vibrate freely.

frisch Fresh, lively.

fuoco Fire.

furioso Furiously.

furore Fury, rage.

ganz Entirely, altogether.

Ganzton Whole tone.

gedämpft (ged.) Muted.

geheimnisvoll Mysteriously.

geschlagen Pulsating.

gestopft (gest.) Stopping the notes of a horn; that is, the hand is placed in the bell of the horn to produce a muffled sound. Also *chiuso.*

geteilt (get.) Divided; indicates that the instrumental group should be divided into two parts to play the passage in question.

getragen Sustained.

gewöhnlich As usual.

giocoso Humorous.

giusto Moderately.

glissando (gliss.) Rapid scales produced by running the fingers over all the strings.

gradamente Gradually.

grande Large, great.

grandezza Grandeur.

grandioso Grandiose.

grave Slow, solemn; deep, low.

grazioso Gracefully.

Griffbrett Fingerboard.

grosser Auftakt Big upbeat.

gut Good, well.

Hälfte Half.

harmonics Individual, pure sounds that are part of a musical tone; on string instruments, crystalline tones in the very high register, produced by lightly touching a vibrating string at a certain point.

Hauptzeitmass Original tempo.

hauteur réelle In the octave notated, designation for transposing French horns.

head The tune and chord progression, in jazz.

hervortreten Prominent.

hoch High, nobly.

Holz Woodwinds.

Holzschlägel Wooden drumstick.

im gleichen Rhythmus In the same rhythm.

immer Always.

impalpable Imperceptively.

in Oktaven In octaves.

insensibilmente Slightly, imperceptibly.

intensa Intensely.

istesso tempo Duration of beat remains unaltered despite meter change.

jeté On a string instrument, the bow is thrown so that it bounces on the string with a series of rapid notes.

jeu Playful.

jusqu'à Until.

kadenzieren To cadence.

klagend Lamenting.

kleine Little.

klingen To sound.

komisch bedeutsam Very humorously.

kurz Short.

laissez To allow; *laisser vibrer,* to let vibrate.

langsam Slow.

langsamer Slower.

languendo, langueur Languor.

l'archet See *archet.*

largamente Broadly.

larghetto Slightly faster than largo.

largo A very slow tempo.

lasci, lassen To abandon.

lebhaft Lively.

lebhafter Livelier.

legatissimo A more forceful indication of *legato.*

legato Performed without any perceptible interruption between notes.

légèrement, leggieramente Lightly.

leggierissimo Very light.

leggiero (legg.) Light and graceful.

legno The wood of the bow (*col legno gestrich,* played with the wood).

lent Slow.

lentamente Slowly.

lento A slow tempo (between andante and largo).

l.h. Abbreviation for "left hand."

liricamente Lyrically.

loco Indicates a return to the written pitch, following a passage played an octave higher or lower than written.

loin Distant, faraway.

Luftpause Pause for breath.

lunga Long, sustained.

lusingando Caressing.

ma, mais But.

maestoso Majestic.

mailloche Timpani mallet.

marcatissimo (marcatiss.) With very marked emphasis.

marcato (marc.) Marked, with emphasis.

marcia March.

marschmässig, nicht eilen Moderate-paced march, not rushed.

marziale Military, martial, march-like.

mässig Moderately.

mässiger More moderately.

melodia Melody.

même Same.

meno Less.

mettez With (as in *mettez les sourdines*, with the mutes).

mezzo forte (mf) Moderately loud.

mezzo piano (mp) Moderately soft.

mezzo voce With half voice, restrained.

mindestens At least.

misterioso Mysterious.

misura Measured.

mit With.

moderatissimo A more forceful indication of *moderato*.

moderato, modéré At a moderate tempo.

moins Less.

molto Very, much.

mordenti Biting, pungent.

morendo Dying away.

mormorato Murmured.

mosso Rapid.

moto Motion.

mouvement (mouv., mouvt.) Tempo (as in *au mouvement*, a tempo).

muta, mutano Change the tuning of the instrument as specified.

nach After.

naturalezza A natural, unaffected manner.

nel modo russico In the Russian style.

neuen New.

nicht Not.

niente Nothing.

nimmt To take; to seize.

noch Still.

node A point at which vibrations do not occur.

non Not.

nuovo New.

obere, oberer (ob.) Upper, leading.

oder langsamer Or slower.

offen Open.

ohne Without.

ondeggiante Undulating movement of the bow, which produces a tremolo effect.

open On a French horn, removing the hand or mute.

ordinario (ord., ordin.) In the usual way (generally canceling an instruction to play using some special technique).

ossia An alternative (usually easier) version of a passage.

ôtez vite les sourdines Remove the mutes quickly.

ottava Octave (as in *8va*, octave higher than written; *8 basso, 8 bassa*, octave lower than written; *16 va*, two octaves higher than written).

ottoni Brass.

ouvert Open.

parte Part (*colla parte, colle parti*, the accompaniment is to follow the soloist[s] in tempo).

passionato Passionately.

passione Passion, emotion.

Paukenschlägel Timpani stick.

pavillons en l'air An indication to the player of a wind instrument to raise the bell of the instrument upward.

pedal, pedale (ped., P.) (1) In piano music, indicates that the damper pedal should be depressed; an asterisk indicates the point of release (brackets below the music are also used to indicate pedaling); (2) on an organ, the pedals are a keyboard played with the feet.

per During.

perdant fading (as in *en se perdant*, dying away).

perdendosi Gradually dying away.

pesante Heavily.

peu Little, a little.

piacevole Agreeable, pleasant.

pianissimo (pp) Very soft (*ppp* indicates a still softer dynamic).

piano (p) Soft.

piena Full.

più More.

pizzicato (pizz.) The string plucked with the finger.

plötzlich Suddenly, immediately.

plus More.

pochissimo (pochiss.) Very little, a very little.

poco Little, a little.

poco a poco Little by little.

ponticello (pont.) The bridge (of a string instrument).

portamento Continuous smooth and rapid sliding between two pitches.

portando Carrying.

position naturel (pos. nat.) In the normal position (usually canceling an instruction to play using some special technique).

possibile Possible.

precedente Previous, preceding.

precipitato Rushed, hurried.

premier mouvement (1er mouvt.) At the original tempo.

prenez Take up.

préparez Prepare.

presque Almost, nearly.

presser To speed up.

prestissimo A more forceful indication of *presto*.

presto A very quick tempo (faster than allegro).

prima, primo First, principal.

principale First, principal, solo.

punto Point.

quarta Fourth.

quasi Almost, as if.

quinto Fifth.

ralentissez Slow down.

rallentando (rall., rallent.) Growing slower.

rapidamente Quickly.

rapide Rapid, fast.

rapidissimo (rapidiss.) Very quickly.

rasch Quickly.

rascher More quickly.

rauschend Rustling, roaring.

recitative, recitativo (recit.) A vocal style designed to imitate and emphasize the natural inflections of speech.

rein Perfect interval.

reprenez Take again, put on again.

resonante Resonating.

respiro Pause for breath.

retenu Held back.

revenir au tempo Return to the original tempo.

r.h. Abbreviation for "right hand."

rianimando Reanimating.

richtig Correct (*richtige Lage*, correct pitch).

rien Nothing.

rigore di tempo Strictness of tempo.

rigueur Rigor, strictness.

rinforzando (rf, rfz, rinf.) A sudden accent on a single note or chord.

risoluto In a resolute or determined manner.

ritardando (rit., ritard.) Gradually slackening in speed.

ritenuto (riten.) Immediate reduction of speed.

ritmato, ritmico Rhythmic.

ritornando, ritornello (ritor.) Refrain.

robuste Robustly.

rubato A certain elasticity and flexibility of tempo, consisting of slight accelerandos and ritardandos according to the requirements of the musical expression.

ruhig Quietly.

saltando Leaping.

sans Without.

scat A jazz vocal style that sets syllables without meaning (vocables) to an improvised vocal line.

Schalltrichter Horn.

scherzando (scherz.) Playful.

schlagen To strike in a usual manner.

Schlagwerk Striking mechanism.

schleppen, schleppend Dragging.

Schluss Cadence, conclusion.

schnell Fast.

schneller Faster.

schon Already.

Schwammschägeln Sponge-headed drumstick.

scorrevole Flowing, gliding.

sec, secco Dry, simple.

secunda Second.

sehr Very.

semplice Simple.

semplicità Simplicity.

sempre Always, continually.

senza Without.

sforzando (sf., sfz.) With sudden emphasis.

sforzandissimo (sff, sffz) With very loud, sudden attack.

shake An effect on a brass instrument resembling an exaggerated vibrato, produced by shaking the instrument against the lips while playing; used in jazz.

simile (sim.) In a similar manner.

sin Without.

Singstimme Singing voice.

sino al Up to the . . . (usually followed by a new tempo marking, or by a dotted line indicating a terminal point).

si piace Especially pleasing.

smorzando (smorz.) Dying away.

sofort Immediately.

soli, solo (s.) Executed by one performer.

son naturel Natural sound; on a brass instrument, played without valves.

sonoro Sonorous, resonant.

sopra Above; in piano music, used to indicate that one hand must pass above the other.

soprano (S.) The voice classification with the highest range.

sordini, sordino (sord.) Mute.

sostenendo, sostenuto (sost.) Sustained.

sotto voce In an undertone, subdued, under the breath.

sourdine (sourd.) Mute.

soutenu Sustained.

spiel, spielen Play (an instrument).

Spieler Player, performer.

spirito Spirit, soul.

spiritoso In a spirited manner.

spugna Sponge.

staccato (stacc.) Detached, separated, abruptly, disconnected.

stentando, stentare, stentato (stent.) Delaying, retarding.

stesso The same.

Stimme Voice.

stimmen To tune.

stopped On a French horn, closing the opening of the bell with the hand or a mute.

strascinare To drag.

straziante Agonizing, heart-rending.

Streichinstrumente (Streichinstr.) Bowed string instruments.

strepitoso Noisy, loud.

stretto In a non-fugal composition, indicates a concluding section at an increased speed.

stringendo (string.) Quickening.

subito (sub.) Suddenly, immediately.

suivez Follow (as in *suivez le solo*, follow the solo line).

sul On the (as in *sul G*, on the G string).

superius In older music, the uppermost part.

sur On.

tacet The instrument or vocal part so marked is silent.

tasto Fingerboard (as in *sul tasto*, bow over the fingerboard).

tasto solo In a continuo part, this indicates that only the string instrument plays; the chord-playing instrument is silent.

tema Theme.

tempo primo (tempo I) At the original tempo.

teneramente, tenero Tenderly, gently.

tenor, tenore (T.) The highest male voice.

tenuto (ten., tenu.) Held, sustained.

tertia Third.

tief Deep, low.

timbre Tone color.

touche Key; note; fingerboard (as in *sur la touche*, on the fingerboard).

toujours Always, continually.

tranquillo Quietly, calmly.

tre corde (t.c.) Release the soft (or *una corda*) pedal of the piano.

tremolo (trem.) On string instruments, a quick reiteration of the same tone, produced by a rapid up-and-down movement of the bow; also a rapid alternation between two different notes.

très Very.

trill (tr.) The rapid alternation of a given note with the diatonic second above it. In a drum part, it indicates rapid alternating strokes with two drumsticks.

tromba Trumpet (as in *quasi tromba*, trumpet-like).

Trommschlag (Tromm.) Drumbeat.

troppo Too much.

tutta la forza Very emphatically.

tutti Literally, "all"; usually means all the instruments in a given category as distinct from a solo part.

übergreifen To overlap.

übertonend Drowning out.

umstimmen To change the tuning.

un One, a.

una corda (u.c.) With the "soft" pedal of the piano depressed.

und And.

unison (unis.) The same notes or melody played by several instruments at the same pitch. Often used to emphasize that a phrase is not to be divided among several players.

unmerklich Imperceptible.

velocissimo Very swiftly.

verklingen lassen To let die away.

vibrare, vibrer To sound, vibrate.

vibrato (vibr.) To fluctuate the pitch on a single note.

vierfach Quadruple.

vierhändig Four-hand piano music.

vif Lively.

vigoroso Vigorous, strong.

violento Violent.

viva, vivente, vivo Lively.

vivace Quick, lively.

vivacissimo A more forceful indication of *vivace*.

voce Voice (as in *colla voce*, a direction for the accompaniment to follow the solo part in tempo and expression).

volles Orch. Entire orchestra.

vorbereiten Prepare, get ready.

Vorhang auf Curtain up.

Vorhang zu Curtain down.

vorher Beforehand, previously.

voriges Preceding.

Waltzertempo In the tempo of a waltz.

weg Away, beyond.

weich Mellow, smooth, soft.

wie aus der Fern As if from afar.

wieder Again.

wie zu Anfang dieser Szene As at the beginning of this scene.

zart Tenderly, delicately.

Zeit Time; duration.

zögernd Slower.

zu The phrases *zu 2, zu 3* (etc.) indicate the number of parts to be played by 2, 3 (etc.) players.

zum In addition.

zurückhaltend Slackening in speed.

zurücktreten To withdraw.

zweihändig With two hands.

Appendix D

Concordance Table for Recordings and Listening Guides

The following table provides cross-references to the Listening Guides (LG) in *The Enjoyment of Music,* eighth edition, by Joseph Machlis and Kristine Forney (New York: Norton, 1999). The following abbreviations are used throughout: *Chr* for the Chronological version, *Std* for the Standard version, and *Sh* for the Shorter version. The table also gives the location of each work on the various recordings sets (see "A Note on the Recordings," p. xiv). An asterisk (*) indicates inclusion in *The Norton CD-ROM MasterWorks,* vol. I.

LISTENING GUIDES

CHR PAGE	STD PAGE	SH PAGE	COMPOSER, TITLE	SCORE PAGE	8-CD SET	8-CAS SET	4-CD SET	4-CAS SET
342	83	281	SCHUBERT, *Erlkönig (Erlking),* D. 328*	1	5/1	5A/1	3/6	3A/2
321	317	—	SCHUBERT, *Die Forelle (The Trout),* D. 550	8	5/9	5A/2	—	—
322	318	—	SCHUBERT, Quintet in A major for Piano and Strings (*Trout*), D. 667, fourth movement	14	5/12	5A/3	—	—
379	120	304	BERLIOZ, *Symphonie fantastique*	30				
379	120	304	Fourth movement, *Marche au supplice (March to the Scaffold)*	30	5/31	5B/1	3/30	3B/1
380	121	—	Fifth movement, *Songe d'une nuit du sabbat (Dream of a Witches' Sabbath)*	51	5/37	5B/2	—	—

<u>LISTENING GUIDES</u>

CHR PAGE	STD PAGE	SH PAGE	COMPOSER, TITLE	SCORE PAGE	8-CD SET	8-CAS SET	4-CD SET	4-CAS SET
644	646	—	LUTOSŁAWSKI, *Jeux vénitiens (Venetian Games)*, first movement	775	8/14	8A/3	—	—
592	594	438	BERNSTEIN, *West Side Story*	780				
593	595	439	*Mambo*	780	8/19	8A/5	4/40	4A/8
593	595	439	*Tonight* Ensemble	803	8/22	8A/6	4/43	4A/9
653	655	485	LIGETI, *Désordre (Disorder)*, from *Etudes for Piano*, Book I	819	8/30	8A/7	4/64	4B/2
640	642		BOULEZ, *Le marteau sans maître (The Hammer Without a Master)*	824				
640	642	—	No. 1. *Avant "L'artisanat furieux" (Before "Furious Artisans")*	824	8/37	8A/9	—	—
641	643	—	No. 3. *L'artisanat furieux (Furious Artisans)*	830	8/38	8A/10	—	—
642	644	—	No. 7. *Après "L'artisanat furieux" (After "Furious Artisans")*	833	8/39	8A/11	—	—
650	652	482	CRUMB, *Ancient Voices of Children*, first movement, *El niño busca su voz (The Little Boy Is Looking for His Voice)*	837	8/40	8A/12	4/61	4B/1
685	687	514	REICH, *City Life*, first movement, "Check it out"	840	8/43	8B/1	4/84	4B/7
661	663	493	UNG, *Spiral*, excerpt	885	8/49	8B/2	4/71	4B/4
673	675	—	LANSKY, *Notjustmoreidlechatter*, excerpt	892	8/59	8B/4	—	—
678	680	508	LARSEN, *Symphony: Water Music*, first movement, *Fresh Breeze*	894	8/63	8B/5	4/81	4B/6
665	667	497	ABING (HUA YANJUN), Chinese traditional music: *Er quan ying yue (The Moon Reflected on the Second Springs)*	931	8/55	8B/3	4/77	4B/5
610	612	456	IRISH TRADITIONAL DANCES, *The Wind That Shakes the Barley* and *The Reel with the Beryle*	932	8/66	8B/6	4/51	4A/10

Acknowledgments

Page 8: Franz Schubert, *Die Forelle,* D. 550, from Schubert, *Lieder I, Sopran oder Tenor.* Used by permission of C. F. Peters Corporation. **Page 14:** Franz Schubert, Quintet in A Major (the *Trout*), D. 667. Edited by Anke Butzer and Jurgen Neubacher. © 1988 Ernst Eulenburg Ltd. All rights reserved. Used by permission of European American Music Distributors Corporation, sole U.S. and Canadian agent for Ernst Eulenburg Ltd. **Page 105:** Fanny Mendelssohn Hensel, *Bergeslust,* Op. 10, No. 5, from Fanny Mendelssohn Hensel, *Ausgewählte Lieder für Singstimme und Klavier,* edited by Annette Maurer, vol. 1, no. 12 (1993–94). Copyright by Breitkopf & Härtel, Wiesbaden. Reprinted by permission. **Page 110:** Felix Mendelssohn, Violin Concerto, Op. 64. Used by permission of European American Music Distributors Corporation, sole U.S. and Canadian agent for Ernst Eulenburg Ltd. **Page 170:** Robert Schumann, *Dichterliebe,* Op. 48, No. 8 "Und wüssten's die Blumen," from C. F. Peters No. 2383a, *Lieder I, Original-Ausgabe.* Used by permission of C. F. Peters Corporation. **Page 183:** Richard Wagner, *Die Walküre,* Act III, Finale. Translation by Frederick Jameson and Andrew Porter. Copyright © 1936 (renewed) by G. Schirmer, Inc. (ASCAP). International copyright secured. All rights reserved. Reprinted by permission. **Page 193:** Giuseppe Verdi, *Rigoletto,* Act III: "La donna è mobile" and "Un di, se ben rammentomi" (Quartet). Copyright © 1957 (renewed) by G. Schirmer, Inc. (ASCAP). International copyright secured. All rights reserved. Reprinted by permission. **Page 217:** Clara Schumann, Scherzo, Op. 10, from *Clara Wieck-Schumann: Ausgewählte Klavierwerke.* Copyright by G. Henle Verlag. Reprinted by permission. **Page 291:** Johannes Brahms, *Ein deutsches Requiem (A German Requiem),* fourth movement. From Edition Peters No. 3672. Used by permission of C. F. Peters Corporation. **Page 302:** Johannes Brahms, Symphony No. 3. Used by permission of European American Music Distributors Corporation, sole U.S. and Canadian agent for Ernst Eulenburg Ltd. **Page 355:** Georges Bizet, *Carmen,* Act I: scenes 3–5, English translation by Ruth and Thomas Martin, Copyright © 1958 (renewed) by G. Schirmer, Inc. (ASCAP). International copyright secured. All rights reserved. Reprinted by permission. **Page 436:** Antonín Dvořák, Symphony No. 9. Edited by Klaus Doege. © 1986 Ernst Eulenburg Ltd. All rights reserved. Used by permission of European American Music Distributors Corporation, sole U.S. and Canadian agent for Ernst Eulenburg Ltd. **Page 454:** Ruggero Leoncavallo, *Pagliacci,* Act I: Canio's Aria. English translation by Ruth and Thomas Martin. Copyright © 1960 (renewed) by G. Schirmer, Inc. (ASCAP). International copyright secured. All rights reserved. Reprinted by permission. **Page 459:** Gustav Mahler, *Das Lied von der Erde (The Song of the Earth).* Copyright 1912 by Universal Edition A.G., Wien. Copyright renewed, assigned 1952 to Universal Edition (London) Ltd., London. © This edition,

952

revised by the Internationale Gustav-Mahler-Gesellschaft, copyright 1962 by Universal Edition A.G., Wien, and Universal Edition (London) Ltd., London. © renewed. All rights reserved. Used by permission of European American Music Distributors Corporation, sole U.S. and Canadian agent for Universal Edition A.G., Wien, and Universal Edition (London) Ltd., London. **Page 501:** Richard Strauss, *Der Rosenkavalier*. Text by Hugo von Hofmannsthal. © 1911 by Furstner for Germany, Italy, Portugal, and the former countries of Russia. Boosey & Hawkes Ltd. for all other countries. © Copyright 1910, 1911 by Adolph Furstner. U.S. copyright renewed. Copyright assigned 1943 by Hawkes & Son (London) Ltd. (a Boosey & Hawkes Company) for the world excluding Germany, Italy, Portugal, and the Former Territories of the USSR (excluding Estonia, Latvia, and Lithuania). Reprinted by permission of Boosey & Hawkes, Inc. and European American Music.

Page 521: Arnold Schoenberg, *Pierrot lunaire*, No. 18 and No. 21. Used by permission of Belmont Music Publishers, Pacific Palisades, CA 90272. **Page 531:** Charles Ives, *The Things Our Fathers Loved*, from *Fourteen Songs*. © Copyright 1955 by Peer International Corporation. Reprinted by permission. **Page 534:** Maurice Ravel, *Rapsodie espagnole*. © 1908 Durand S.A. Editions Musicales Editions A.R.I.M.A. & Durand S.A. Editions Musicales. Joint publication. Used by permission. Sole agent U.S.A. Theodore Presser Company. **Page 585:** Béla Bartók, *Concerto for Orchestra*, © Copyright 1946 by Hawkes & Son (London) Ltd. Copyright renewed. Reprinted by permission of Boosey & Hawkes, Inc. **Page 596:** Igor Stravinsky, *Petrouchka*. © Copyright 1912 by Hawkes & Son (London) Ltd. Copyright renewed. Revised version © copyright 1948 by Hawkes & Son (London) Ltd. Copyright renewed. Reprinted by permission of Boosey & Hawkes, Inc. **Page 652:** Anton Webern, Symphony, Op. 21. Copyright 1929 by Universal Edition. Copyright renewed. All rights reserved. Used by permission of European American Music Distributors Corporation, sole U.S. and Canadian agent for Universal Edition. **Page 660:** Alban Berg, *Wozzeck*. Full score copyright 1926 by Universal Edition A.G., Vienna. Full score copyright renewed. English translation copyright 1952 by Alfred A. Kalmus, London. English translation copyright renewed. All rights reserved. Used by permission of European American Music Distributors Corporation, sole U.S. and Canadian agent for Universal Edition A.G., Vienna. **Page 685:** Sergei Prokofiev, *Alexander Nevsky*. From the *Alexander Nevsky* Cantata, Op. 78, for chorus and orchestra, by Sergei Prokofiev. Copyright © 1941 (renewed) by G. Schirmer, Inc. (ASCAP). International copyright secured. All rights reserved. Reprinted by permission. **Page 698:** Lillian Hardin Armstrong, *Hotter Than That*. © Copyright 1928 by MCA Music Publishing, a division of Universal Studios, Inc. Copyright renewed. International copyright secured. All rights reserved. Reprinted by permission of Hal Leonard Corporation. **Page 700:** Duke Ellington, *Ko-Ko*. © 1940 (renewed) EMI Robbins Catalog Inc. All rights reserved. Used by permission. Warner Bros. Publications U.S. Inc., Miami, FL. 33014.

Page 719: Aaron Copland, *Billy the Kid*. © Copyright 1941 by The Aaron Copland Fund for Music, Inc. Copyright renewed. Reprinted by permission of Boosey & Hawkes, Inc., sole licensee. **Page 760:** Richard Rodgers and Lorenz Hart, *My Funny Valentine*: words by Lorenz Hart, music by Richard Rodgers. Copyright © 1937 by Williamson Music and The Estate of Lorenz Hart in the United States. Copyright renewed. All rights on behalf of The Estate of Lorenz Hart administered by WB Music Corp. International copyright secured. All rights reserved. © 1937 (renewed) Chappell & Co. Rights for extended renewal term in U.S. controlled by The Estate of Lorenz Hart (administered by WB Music Corp.) and Family Trust U/W Richard Rodgers and the Estate of Dorothy F. Rodgers (administered by Williamson Music). All rights reserved. Used by permission. Warner Bros. Publications U.S. Inc., Miami, FL. 33014. 1953 recording of Gerry Mulligan's Quartet Version of *My Funny Valentine* transcribed by Evan Solot. **Page 767:** Olivier Messiaen, *Quartet for the End of Time*, ©1942 Durand S.A. Used by permission. Sole agent U.S.A. Theodore Presser Company. **Page 775:** Witold Lutosławski, *Jeux Venitiens"* © 1962 by Moeck Verlag, Celle © renewed. All rights reserved. Used by permission of European American Music Distributors Corporation, sole U.S. and Canadian agent for Moeck Verlag, Celle. **Page 780:** Leonard Bernstein, *West Side Story,* selections. © Copyright 1956, 1957 by The Estate of Leonard Bernstein and Stephen Sondheim. Copyright renewed. Reprinted by permission of Leonard Bernstein Music Publishing Company LLC, Publisher, and Boosey & Hawkes, Inc., sole agent. **Page 819:** György Ligeti, *Etudes Pour Piano, Premiere Livre,* © B. Schott's Soehne, Mainz, 1986. All rights reserved. Used by permission of European American Music Distributors Corporation, sole U.S. and Canadian agent for B. Schott's Soehne, Mainz. **Page 824:** Pierre Boulez, *Le marteau sans maitre* . © Copyright 1954 by Universal Edition (London) Ltd., London. Final version: © Copyright 1957 by Universal Edition (London) Ltd., London. © Copyrights renewed. *Poems de René Char.* © Copyright 1964 by Jose Corti Editeur, Paris. © Copyright renewed. All rights reserved. Used by permission of European American Music Distributors Corporation, sole U.S. and Canadian agent for Universal Edition (London) Ltd., London. **Page 837:** George Crumb, *Ancient Voices of Children,* first movement, *El niño busca su voz.* Copyright © 1970 by C. F. Peters Corporation, 373 Park Avenue South, New York, NY 10016. Reprinted with permission of the publishers who published the score of the complete work under Peters Edition No. 66303. **Page 840:** Steve Reich, *City Life.* © Copyright 1994, 1998 by Hendon Music Inc., a Boosey & Hawkes company. Reprinted by permission. **Page 885:** Chinary Ung, *Spiral,* excerpt. Copyright © 1989 by C. F. Peters Corporation, 373 Park Avenue South, New York, NY 10016. International copyright secured. All rights reserved. **Page 892:** Paul Lansky, *Notjustmoreidlechatter.* Copyright © 1998 by GrimTim Music. **Page 894:** Libby Larsen, *Symphony: Water Music,* first movement. Copyright 1984 by E. C. Schirmer Music Co. Inc., for all countries. A division of ECS Publishing.

TRANSLATIONS:

Page 682: Alban Berg, *Wozzeck,* translation by Sarah E. Soulsby. See acknowledgment above. **Page 839:** Federico García Lorca, *El niño busca su voz,* from *Obras Completas* (Galaxia Gutenberg, 1996 edition), © Herederos de Federico García Lorca. Translation by W. S. Merwin, © W. S. Merwin and Herederos de Federico García Lorca. All rights reserved. For information regarding rights and permissions for works by Federico García Lorca, please contact William Peter Kosmas, Esq., 8 Franklin Square, London W14 9UU, England. Reprinted by permission.

Index of Forms and Genres